SUBURBAN
LEGEND

A MEMOIR

LCCN Library of Congress Control Number: 2021911742
ISBN 978-1-7373806-0-3 (paperback)
ISBN 978-1-7373806-1-0 (ebook)

Cover design by Willy Eddy
Cover illustration by Daniela Olaru
Layout design by Taylor Roy

First Edition
Published by Girl Noise Press
girlnoise.net

SUBURBAN LEGEND

A MEMOIR

by

Diana Le

GIRL NOISE

PRESS

CONTENTS

To my younger self. You're gonna be just fine.

NOTE

Most of the essays in this book were first written in 2019. By the time this book comes out, the girl who wrote this book no longer exists. Nor do a lot of the people she writes about. She hopes this book will change her. And her perceptions of the people she wrote about.

Lê Ngọc Anh

∎

Childhood

∎

I conducted this interview as part of a college assignment. I was 20 years old at the time. The class was called Testimony and Allegory in World Literature, and the course description stated: *How do texts and films describe cataclysmic and traumatic events? How does the narrator cope with the need to tell and retell painful experiences? How do authors address not only the past but also the present in which they are producing their work?* For our final project, we had to "interview a friend or a family member about an important event that has involved some loss."

So in February of 2012, I interviewed my mother.

*This interview has been translated from Vietnamese.

■

CAN I PLEASE HAVE YOU STATE YOUR NAME?
Ann Martin.

AND IS THAT THE NAME YOU WERE BORN WITH?
No, I was born with my Vietnamese name,[1] which is Lê Ngọc Anh.

WHEN AND WHERE WERE YOU BORN?
I was born in 1962 in Quang Ngai,[2] Vietnam.

WHAT IS YOUR EARLIEST CHILDHOOD MEMORY?
I think it was in preschool. I was attending the same school as your third and your fourth aunt.[3] They were older than me. I liked the ends or the "butts" of loaves of bread. They were crunchy. Normally, people would eat up until that part and throw them away. But because I was in preschool, I

1
My Vietnamese name is Na.
2
A city in central Vietnam.

3
In Vietnamese culture, we typically refer to siblings and relatives by their birth order to denote their age and relationship within the family. We start counting at two, rather than one. So the firstborn is #2, the second born is #3, and so on.

picked up someone's leftover crust and ate it. And either your third or your fourth aunt came over to pick me up and saw me. They went home and told the rest of the family, and they still tell that story to this day [laughs].

WHAT WERE THE SCHOOLS LIKE?

Our family moved to Nha Trang because of Grandpa's job. We moved there after Lunar New Year. The school there was poor, it's not like over here. But because we always lived in cities and not rural areas, in Vietnam this school was considered nice. The schools were normally constructed very simply. There was a blackboard where we wrote with chalk.

In Vietnam, we went to school for half a day. You either went to school in the morning or the afternoon because the school wasn't big enough. We didn't go to school a full day like they do here.

WHAT WOULD YOU LEARN IN SCHOOL?

From first grade to fifth grade, we learned general science, math, vocabulary, geography, history.

WERE YOU REQUIRED TO LEARN A FOREIGN LANGUAGE? DID YOU LEARN ENGLISH?

Yes. My first foreign language was English.

DID YOU FIND IT DIFFICULT?

No. When I was living in Saigon, the school I was attending was a school built by the British. So I had been learning English since third or fourth grade. Normally, you didn't start learning English until middle school, but my elementary school taught it because that school was built by the British for Vietnam.

WHAT WAS YOUR NEIGHBORHOOD LIKE? DID YOU GO OUTSIDE OF YOUR NEIGHBORHOOD A LOT?

No, normally all of your schoolmates lived really close to you. All our friends were really close. I also was a part of a group through the temple. It wasn't Girl Scouts, but it was something similar to that. We were like scouts to the religion. We also went camping.

CAN YOU TELL ME ABOUT YOUR PARENTS? WHAT WERE THEIR PROFESSIONS?

My dad—Grandpa, taught mathematics and science for high school and college. Grandma just stayed at home and cooked. She was a housewife.[4]

HOW DID THEY RAISE THEIR CHILDREN?

Grandpa was very strict. It was very difficult. If we wanted to go somewhere we had to ask permission. And in Vietnam, the expectation was that you only moved out of the house when you got married. It's not like here where you can move out when you become of age.

HOW MANY SIBLINGS DO YOU HAVE?

Including me, seven. I have two brothers and four sisters.[5]

WHEN YOU AND YOUR SIBLINGS WERE YOUNG, WHAT DID YOU LIKE TO DO FOR FUN?

Your sixth aunt and I were close in age, two years apart, so we were very close. We played hopscotch, jump rope, and I don't know what you call it, we would let go of a ball and grab...What is that called?

OH, JACKS?

Yeah, I tended to play that a lot. And we also liked to play with dolls. But it wasn't like here, there weren't very many dolls. Only very rich families could afford to buy dolls. So if you couldn't afford to buy dolls, you would have to make them yourself by cutting out doll shapes and clothing from paper and coloring them in.

DIANA LE

4

My grandma married when she was sixteen, and as per Vietnamese tradition, she had to move in with my grandpa and his parents and cook and clean for them until they started having children of their own.

Her life was very difficult. My grandpa cheated on her a lot. He was a young, handsome teacher and his female students would often show up at the house looking for him.

My grandma now has dementia, and as it progresses, she seems to be mentally trapped in this time. When I visited her last, she spoke about it as if it were happening now. She would see one of my uncles walk by and mistake them for my grandpa. She'd say, "I know you don't love me anymore. You don't come home at night. You're always leaving."

5

My mom is the fourth born out of her seven siblings. A middle child, like me.

■

Sad Girl Media Diet

■

Emo Music

Growing up, I had a lot of things to be sad about—you'll learn about those things later—but I never talked about them. I went to school and tried to be normal. Then my mom married Bill and he became my stepdad and I had a lot more to be sad about. In middle school, my friends and I discovered emo music. And we quickly adopted the style and the culture. For the first time, it felt okay to be sad. I still didn't really talk about why I was sad, but I was able to express my sadness through the way I looked. Kohl-rimmed eyes, chokers that looked like dog collars, band tees, studded belts, Converse with song lyrics written on the sidewalls in Sharpie. I was seeing the world through one eye (because the other eye was obviously obstructed by heavy, side-swept bangs).

Dark YA Books

In middle school, I read YA books about partying and drugs and suicide and self-harm and sexual assault. Books like *Girl*, *Go Ask Alice*, *The Burn Journals*, *Cut*, and *Speak*. I was curious about those experiences but I didn't want to experience them myself. If anything, I took them as cautionary tales. But I connected with the pain and sadness of the characters. It made me feel less crazy, like maybe the authors of these books experienced those things and they grew up and were okay now.

I think I finally told my mom how sad I was at some point. She took me to the doctor and he prescribed me some sort of antidepressant. I took it for a while but I couldn't tell if it was helping so I never asked my mom to refill the prescription. Then some crazy stuff went down with my family and I was diagnosed with an "adjustment disorder" so I had to go to counseling. I went to the same counselor on and off until I was eighteen, when my counselor moved to a clinic that didn't take my insurance.

Mixtapes

In high school, I stopped being emo and started dressing normal. But it was probably the saddest I'd ever been. After reading *High Fidelity* and *Love Is a Mix Tape*, I spent all my time making mixtapes and mix CDs, sandwiching a Paramore song between a Beastie Boys song and an Otis Redding song. I mostly made them for my boyfriend and for driving around in my old Mustang 5.0 that was always breaking down and that I only bought because my stepdad pressured me, insisting that it was cool and iconic. When it'd break down on the side of the road, I'd call him and he'd tell me to figure it out and hang up. There were times I was driving and couldn't shake the thought of swerving right into oncoming traffic. I'd drive home from school and just sit in the driveway and listen to my mixes because I didn't want to go inside and face my stepdad. It got so bad that I started taking over-the-counter sleeping pills every night just so I could escape my own thoughts. But the sleep was never good. I'd wake up groggy and disoriented. I'd pound a huge gas station coffee and then head to school. I was the walking dread.

BORN TO DIE BY LANA DEL REY (ALBUM, 2012)

College was an extremely lonely and confusing time. I spent a lot of my time alone in my tiny, shitty room in a tiny, shitty basement where the bathroom was in the kitchen. I started noticing something happening online. Girls were talking about being sad. It was like everyone had just learned the term "existential crisis" all at once. So I started tweeting about being sad:

i wish this was harry potter and the darkness could be cured with chocolate

was going to share an embarrassingly self-revealing blog post filled with RAW EMOTION but then my internet stopped working.

My secret to staying skinny: being sad. As we know, it takes more muscles to frown than it does to smile.

How many calories does crying burn?

so good at disguising self-hatred as self-deprecation that everyone at work just thinks i'm doing a bit.

what am i doing boiling water for my couscous when i don't know why i exist.

The only thing currently tethering me to the world is 9 seasons of X-files. But probably the weight I've gained. #cookies

feeling emo, but want to party.

I am Jack's suppressed emotions.

I've stopped believing in the end result. #school #20somethingcrisis

I mean, does it really matter if I finish my film studies degree?

I became a capital S, capital G *Sad Girl*. I listened to Lana Del Ray and read *The Journals of Sylvia Plath*. I even decorated my bedroom like the girls in *The Virgin Suicides*. And I identified way too much with this quote from *Meridian* by Alice Walker: "...she was considered approaching beautiful only when she looked sad."

For the first time since being emo in middle school, it felt like it was cool to be sad. Or at least okay. And it wasn't about looking sad, it was about talking about being sad.

FRINGE (TV SERIES, 2008–2013)

By junior year, I thought I wanted to work in film, so I switched my major from Cinema Studies to CineMedia. It was this new pilot program with a focus on film production. There were only ten of us in the cohort, and the program director created classes just for us. There was one class where we worked with the upper-level acting students to recreate scenes from *Twin Peaks*. And another class where we analyzed *Vertigo* for the entire quarter. We'd hang out and go to screenings together. I felt like I was in this secret club.

But it was hard. One of our assignments was to write a script for a five-minute short. A new guy had just joined the program. He read his script for the group and it was this broad, cliché story about a guy whose wife died and she was a ghost haunting their home or some shit like that. And our program director thought it was just the greatest and was treating this new guy like he was a genius and would definitely be the next best thing. I read my script about a group of girls at a dinner party who all get their period at the same time around the dining table and then something happens, and they start fighting in a very Tarantino meets Edgar Wright kind of way. Everyone hated it.

I couldn't stand the thought of another year and a half in the program and the teacher's pet and working with boys that told me they didn't want to work with me because I was a girl, and doing something I was obviously bad at. And did I even like film production? Maybe I should transfer to an actual film school. Maybe I just didn't like working with other people. I was lost and depressed again. I needed a break.

I dropped all my classes, told the program director I was leaving the program, and moved back in with my parents, where I hadn't lived since I'd left prematurely at seventeen.

I tried to fake productivity at first. I looked into transferring to UCLA but never followed through. Then I started applying for jobs. I got an interview at a photography studio but I called the lady a few days before my interview and canceled it.

My mom and my Bill would leave for work, my kid sister Andrea would leave for school, and I'd lie in bed and watch *Fringe*, a sci-fi show about a division of the FBI that investigates unexplained occurrences and alternate universes. I wondered what Alt Diana was doing with her life and if she was happy.

I watched it all day. I'd leave my room to eat dinner and then I'd go back to my room and keep watching *Fringe*. I could hear my mom and Bill talking and arguing about me from the living room. My mom would stand in my doorway and tell me to get up and ask me what my plan was. I just told her to leave and I kept watching *Fringe*.

That's all I remember from that time. Watching *Fringe* and fighting with my mom and hating Bill and lying in bed so long that I developed back pain.

After I finished *Fringe*, I didn't know what to do with myself. And I couldn't stand being around my parents anymore, so I decided to go back to school.

DAWSON'S CREEK (TV SERIES, 1998–2003)

Senior year of college, I broke up with my boyfriend, Dylan, and started dating his best friend, John. I was living in my own version of a teen soap opera. Around the same time, I started watching *Dawson's Creek*. I had no idea about the whole Dawson-Joey-Pacey love triangle thing. It fucked me up.

Like Dawson, Dylan was kind and gentle. He was harmless. Like Pacey, John was funny and sarcastic with a touch of darkness. And like Joey, I was damaged and confused.

Both boys were sad. Dylan's sadness was angsty and mopey. John's sadness was deep and inherent. It felt closer to my own sadness.

Watching my love triangle drama play out on the show as I was living through it was deeply disturbing yet extremely comforting. When Joey and Pacey end up together and Dawson is happy in his own right, I felt hopeful that things would work out for me.

After graduating a quarter late because of my mid-college crisis, my job at the campus library let me stay on and work full-time through the fall quarter while I found something else. My job there was ending in mid-December and I had two part-time jobs lined up to start in February. I would work as a teacher's assistant at a Montessori preschool in the mornings and as the Calendar Assistant at *Seattle Weekly* in the afternoons. So I had a month and a half off with no school and no work for the first time since I was fifteen. It was gonna be great and restorative!

But it was actually really lonely and depressing. All my friends were either graduated and working full-time jobs or still in school. My boyfriend, John, was still in school. So I was all alone during the days with nothing to do.

John would come visit me after class and we'd watch TV and eat cookies and french fries. Then one night he told me that I had a sad girl aesthetic and that he only came over to hang out with me every night because he felt bad for me and like he had to.

I thought that was unfair because he's actually the saddest person I've ever met. And I always let him be sad.

And maybe the online version of my sadness was a little performative. It was definitely a more heightened, self-deprecating version of my sadness. My sadness offline was a lot more debilitating and self-loathing. It looked like me getting ready for class, hair done, make-up on, and completely dressed and looking in the mirror and just hating everything about myself and crawling back into bed and skipping all my classes because I couldn't stand the thought of being seen by anyone. It looked like me eating couscous and broccoli with the same dirty bowl and spoon every day. It looked like me watching *The Devil Wears Prada* three times in one day. It looked like me wandering to the dollar store in the middle of the day in my pajamas and eating a bag of chips on the street and a police officer asking me if I was okay.

After John said that, I stopped performing my sadness on the internet. I stopped performing it in the world. I stopped showing him my real sadness. I stopped showing it to anyone.

Lê Ngọc Anh

■

The War

■

AT WHAT AGE DID YOU BECOME AWARE OF THE WAR? DID GRANDMA AND GRANDPA DISCUSS IT VERY MUCH?

In the year 1968, I was still very young. But that was the year of the Tết Offensive, when North Vietnam attacked Saigon. That was the start of a lot of gunfire in the city. I don't remember it well, but I've heard stories.

THAT WAS HAPPENING IN YOUR CITY?

Yes, in Saigon. Then after that year, Grandpa joined the military. He went to teach in the naval school. So his job moved him out to Nha Trang. The city was a military base. This was in '68. I moved around schools and houses a lot because of his job with the military. Later on, when he was no longer with the military, we left the base and returned to Saigon in 1972.

And in '75 is when the government changed to communism. April of 1975. I first started to really learn about the war as more and more cities were being lost. I became really aware in 1974. Because I lived in Saigon, which hadn't really been affected yet. So in '75 after the Fall of Saigon, then I started to pay attention to the news reports. Because I was so young, I didn't believe that the people in the North, the Viet Cong, were the same as us. I didn't understand. I thought they were different people from a different nation.

I THOUGHT THE VIET CONG WERE PEOPLE IN THE SOUTH WHO HAD DISAFFECTED.

No, they were the North. It was people in the North who followed cộng sản, which means communism. So they were called Viet Cong. And down here we lived in a democracy, and life was easier. And the people's lives up there were more difficult because they followed cộng sản. So cities started falling because they went fighting through here, and South Vietnam lost because the Americans pulled out and there was no one supporting us. So we lost.

DID YOU HAVE ANY FRIENDS OR WERE IN CONTACT WITH ANYONE THAT SIDED WITH THE NORTH?

Well, before '75, I was a part of a drama group that would perform songs and dances. There was one girl who I was acquainted with...

DIANA LE

I was in the sixth grade. So there was this girl that I performed with, but what I didn't realize was that we were learning Viet Cong songs. It wasn't until after '75 that I realized [it]. There were a lot of people who lived in the South but belonged to a different party. They followed the North and they were working undercover in the South. So they would spread their message through these songs and dances. I didn't know, so I would sing along.

AND WERE YOUR PARENTS AWARE THAT YOU WERE DOING THIS?

No, I was just going out to sing and dance. It didn't have any effect on politics. The point is, I was acquainted with this family, but I didn't know. Grandpa also knew a lot of people that were undercover but we didn't know. It wasn't until '75 that these people started coming out with important roles and jobs because they first worked for a different government. And that's how they were so successful in winning and taking over. When it ended there were already people on the inside. These people would go to school and work like normal, but followed a different party.

■

I Wanna Be Stronger
Than Your Dad Was
for Your Mom

■

1. "Wake Me Up When September Ends" by Green Day

2. "You're So Last Summer" by Taking Back Sunday

3. "Dissolve and Decay" by Hawthorne Heights

4. "Temper Temper" by Envy on the Coast

5. "A Wolf in Sheep's Clothing" by This Providence

6. "The Taste of Ink" by The Used

7. "Poison Apple" by Coretta Scott

8. "Such Small Hands" by La Dispute

9. "Love is Murder" by Drop Dead, Gorgeous

10. "Santa Monica" by The Front Bottoms

11. "Welcome to Paradise" by Green Day

■

The summer going into fourth grade, my brother, my
sister, and I were staying in San Jose with our grandma
and relatives like we did every summer break. One day
in August, my aunts and my uncles told us we had to go
home right away. In the car on the way to the airport as
I listened to my brother and my aunt talking, I realized
that my dad had died.

> We were back at my grandma's for the summer. This
> time I was eleven, about to go into the sixth grade. My
> mom called and said she'd been seeing a guy named
> Bill and he was great and he had a dog and it could be
> my dog. I asked her how it could be my dog and she
> said because we were moving in with him.

Two weeks later, we were back in Seattle and he came
over to meet me and my sister Stephanie. He was
white, kind of short, bald, wore a baseball cap, and his
T-shirt tucked into his jeans. He showed me this book

he was lending my mom. The title was *Why Terrorism?* or something like that. And the worst part was, my mom was acting as if she were really interested and excited about it. I wanted to vomit. So I go, "My mom's not gonna be interested in that." I was met with a lot of Sure-I-dos and Of-course-she-doeses. That was the last time we stayed with our grandma over summer break.

Within the week, we were packing to move into his house. He lived in Bothell, Washington, twenty miles from where we were in South Seattle. I was still enrolled in school for a few more days, and being the diligent student that I was, I decided that I was going to keep up with my schoolwork until I had to transfer to my new school. So one afternoon I was sitting on the floor of my bedroom in the basement, doing homework, and my mom comes in and hands me the phone. It's Bill. He's asking me why I wasn't packing up my bedroom. I tell him that I'm doing my homework. He starts yelling and cursing, telling me that I was stupid and that I needed to get to packing immediately. I handed the phone back to my mom in tears.

A few days later, he spent the night. I guess I was supposed to pack up what was in this cupboard we had in our living room. I didn't for some reason. Around ten or eleven that night, Bill storms down the stairs and bursts into my bedroom. He turns on the light and starts screaming at me. Why hadn't I packed up the cupboard like he told me to? I don't know, I just didn't. He screams at me to get up and starts following me out the door and up the stairs, still screaming. I slip on a sheet of paper that had been left on the floor and fall to the ground, hitting the stairs. He must have felt a little bad because he ordered me to go back to bed. I didn't tell my mom about it. But I don't know that it would have changed anything. Pretty soon we were living with him and he was our stepdad or whatever.

I dreaded 2:45pm every day. I spent the ride home on the school bus staring out the window, not wanting to go home. I got off the bus in front of my sister's elementary school where she'd be waiting for me. We'd walk home together, turn on the TV, and divvy up the work. One person would pick up the living room, kitchen counter, and dining room while the other person vacuumed the floor and the stairs. When we got hardwood floors, it switched to sweeping and mopping.

When we finished cleaning, we made ourselves snacks and watched TV. There was never anything good on after school, so we'd settle for *Lilo & Stitch: The Series*, *Recess*, and *Lloyd in Space*. We were always listening for the sound of his car. When we heard the garage door opening, we hid our snacks and braced ourselves. You never knew what mood he'd be in.

Some days he came home jolly and we'd play along, hoping it would last. Other times he came in with a chip on his shoulder and terrorized the family. We'd clean the house exactly the same way every day and sometimes he thought we did a shitty job and would make us do it again or ground us, and some days he decided it was up to his standards.

Bill would eat, then mix himself a drink and settle in front of the TV watching *Cops* or *American Idol*, making fun of "Fantasia Lips Like a Burrito." Stephanie and I would sit at the counter finishing our dinner, divvying up the cleaning. Someone would load the dishwasher and wipe down the counters while the other washed the pots and pans and swept and mopped the floor, including the hallway for some reason. Then if we were lucky, he'd pass out in front of the TV and we were able to slip away to our rooms without being ridiculed or made to sit and watch TV with him. And then we did it again the next day.

Weekends were the worst. Two full days of Bill. Stephanie and I would lay in our respective beds listening for him waking up and calling for us. We were only ever safe when he was asleep. On a good day, we would successfully stay out of his way and he left us alone. Some days he would make us weed and do yard work. Other times he'd make us all go somewhere and spend time as a "family."

After dinner on weekends, Stephanie and I hoped we could sneak away and hang out and talk and watch Disney Channel Original Movies. But sometimes we'd have to play chess with Bill and listen to him call women on whatever show he was watching fat and ugly.

Sometimes my mom would take us to visit our cousins in Burien. We didn't always get to go. Once, he let Stephanie go with my mom but said I had to stay home and pull weeds. My mom started lying about going to see her sister and say that she was running errands or going to the temple or doing her taxes. Whenever we were out and her phone rang, we tensed up, afraid that it would be him. My mom always answered the phone "I'm on my way home," instead of saying hello, in anticipation that he'd start yelling at her for not being home yet.

Pretty soon after we moved in, they told us they were pregnant with my half-sister, Andrea. As her due date got closer, I moved into the bedroom in the basement so the upstairs room could be the nursery. I spent an evening moving some of my things downstairs, starting with all my decor and knick-knacks, taking time to meticulously display things where I wanted. I slept in my bedroom upstairs that night, and early the next morning, I could hear him downstairs in my soon-to-be room. He was yelling that I barely moved anything. Then I heard a lot of banging and crashing. When he left for work, I snuck downstairs and saw that he'd thrown and broken all the belongings I'd spent hours moving the day before, including a small wood sculpture of a house I'd made in shop class that I loved.

Stephanie and I would take the bus to the mall. No matter how far away we were, he'd call and say that if we weren't home in twenty minutes we were grounded. One time as we were running home from the bus stop, I had the idea to rub some dirt on our jeans so we could say we were late because we fell. When we got home he was passed out in front of the TV.

I desperately wished my life could be normal. More like my friends' lives. At school, I tried hard to forget what was going on at home. But sometimes, home found its way to school anyway. Bill expected us to get good grades but was always getting in the way of us doing our assignments. If I needed to type up a school report, he refused to buy new ink for the printer or take me to the library to print it out. He said that when he was in school, they wrote their papers out by hand and why didn't I just do that?

I didn't talk about Bill much to my friends. It was hard to explain and I didn't think they'd understand. Their lives seemed so wholesome. I told them bits and pieces. As far as they knew, my stepdad was just really strict. My friend Emily would complain about her parents, but I thought that was bullshit because her mom paid her for every book she read on top of an allowance. Mine and Stephanie's lives were ruled by housework and we never got an allowance.

We knew no one would understand or even believe us. Because the worst part was, when we were out in public or had company over, he acted all nice and phony and like he was the best dad. He once joked that if a guy wanted to beat his wife and get away with it, all he had to do was hit her in the stomach so it wouldn't show any bruises. This was his way of hitting us in the stomach.

Most nights he'd have two drinks. After a while, he made me mix them for him. A tumbler glass filled two inches below the rim with Smirnoff and the rest was orange juice. It wasn't until I started drinking myself, that I realized cocktails weren't supposed to be five parts alcohol, one part sour.

I always feared that he would somehow take Stephanie away from me. The first year we lived there, Stephanie and I would always try to sleep together. We were frightened and needed each other. She'd sneak out of her bed and into mine once we thought he was asleep across the hall. He would barge into my room most nights and yell at us and make her go back to her room. He forbade us from sleeping together. Stephanie's room shared a wall with mine and there was a small hole in the corner where cable wires were fed through. We tried making a telephone out of plastic cups and the bendy straws Bill used for his screwdrivers so we could talk to each other late at night instead. It didn't really work like how it seemed to in movies and TV. But it was nice to feel connected and know that she was holding onto the other end.

Bill was always trying to separate us, but we'd try to find ways to stay in touch. I was always ordering spy stuff from the Scholastic Book Orders at school. Like invisible ink, so we could write notes to each other. We used walkie-talkies for a little bit, but they made too much noise.

He wouldn't let my mom speak Vietnamese to me and my sister. He would say, "Ching chong ching. You're in America, speak ENGLISH!" She also wasn't allowed to cook Vietnamese food[6] for us, and only did so when he would occasionally go out to the bar to drink instead of from his recliner in front of the television. One morning I woke up to find that he had dumped all our soy sauce down the sink and left the empty bottle out so we'd see it. And he'd thrown our chopsticks in the garbage.

One night he was making meat muffins or something disgusting for dinner and my mom didn't know so she brought home pho[7] takeout. He wouldn't let us eat it. My mom, in one of her rare moments of rebellion, made herself a bowl, sat down, and started eating it. He started screaming at her and she grabbed a plate and threw it past his head, smashing it against the window above the kitchen sink. He called the cops.

6

Xôi Lạp Xưởng

This was my favorite dish as a kid. I always loved when my mom would make it. It's chewy and salty and comforting. As an adult, I've begun asking my mom for her recipes. But she doesn't have anything written out and just cooks from memory and feel, no real measurements. So I came over to watch her make this and just wrote down everything she did. She told me that many street vendors in Vietnam sell this dish and it's really popular with labor workers because of how cheap and filling it is. It's the poor Vietnamese girl's version of rice and beans.

Cook **4 cups sticky rice**

Chop **¼ onion**

Slice **1 package of Chinese sausage** thinly and at a slant

Mince **4 garlic cloves**

When rice is done, stir/fluff it a little in the rice cooker/pot

Heat **½ cup canola/vegetable oil** on high in large pan

Add onion and garlic, and cook until fragrant

Add Chinese sausage

Add **2 tbsp. sugar**

Add **1 ½ cup pork sung** (cooked shredded dried pork)

Add **2 tbsp. black pepper**

Add **½ cup soy sauce**

Add **1 cup fried red onion**

Take off heat before soy sauce completely burns off

Spread rice in a dish or pan in a thin layer (1–1 ½ inch)

Scoop sausage mix on top of rice

Garnish with **green onions**

You can eat it immediately, but definitely let it cool and the flavors soak into the rice before covering and storing.

In those first couple years, I fought back a lot. I talked back and drew attention away from my mom and my sister when they were being antagonized. That made him angrier. Then one day as I sat at the dinner table taking a verbal beating after inserting myself, I looked over at my mom and she just turned away. I realized that my mom never took my side or spoke up for me, so I shut up and stopped standing up for her or myself.

My mom and I were in Stephanie's room with her watching *American Idol* on a tiny TV while I worked on a school report that was due the next day. I think we were trying to avoid Bill. He was mad about something, so he shut off all the power in the house so my mom couldn't watch TV and I couldn't finish my report. He would turn the power back on for thirty seconds at a time, and I would try to write down as much as I could while I could still see my sheet of paper before he shut it off again.

DIANA LE

7

Phở Bò, Chín

When I asked my mom for her pho recipe, she hesitated at first because she thought it would be too complicated to explain to me. But a few days later she texted me the following simplified recipe.

Broth

Beef neck bone (I usually use about 2-3 lb. for a large crockpot)

Small ginger

1 onion (small)

1 Pho Hoa package

- Roast beef neck bone in oven right on the rack at 350 for 10 minutes

- Put all ingredients in slow cooker with full water on low heat, after 6 hours, strain, get broth only. Then season with **fish sauce, salt and pepper** to taste

- Cook **rice noodles** as you would cook pasta

- Prepare **bean sprouts, slice jalapeño, Thai basil, slice yellow onion, chopped green onion** and **cilantro**

To Serve

- Put some cooked rice noodles in the bowl, then layer sliced thin beef eye round (really thin brisket is best, but I've also used thin sliced steak for stir fry) chopped green onions, cilantro, sliced onion...then pour hot broth over

- Serve with bean sprouts, jalapeño, Thai basil, hoisin sauce, sriracha

Enjoy!!

My mom and Bill met at work. Their company was a fruit and vegetable supplier for grocery stores. My mom worked in prep and production and he was the maintenance guy. Every morning when they drove to work together I was terrified my mom would die or he would hurt her and not bring her back. And if she was gone we'd have to live with him alone. I was relieved when after a year, my mom got a job somewhere else and started driving herself to work.

He always wanted to play board games as a family. Monopoly was the worst because he would play the banker and cheat. I accused him of cheating and he said fine, you don't have a bike anymore. He turned and asked Stephanie if she thought he was a cheater. She said yes and he said you don't have a bike anymore either.

I was almost asleep in bed when Bill ripped through my room. I didn't put the leftover baked potatoes away. I protested and said my mom had told me not to. He made me stay up cleaning my room as he supervised. He went to bed an hour in, but I was too afraid to stop until it was spotless. I cleaned until two in the morning. I woke up at six the next day and went to sixth grade.

I was reading *Harry Potter and the Goblet of Fire* in my room and Bill was cleaning the house (which was a rare occurrence) and playing his classic rock super loud. I went outside and read on the lawn, hoping it'd be a little quieter. It only took a few minutes for him to find me. He grabbed my book and started yelling at me to get back to my room. I didn't get my book back until the next morning.

My mom and I were out grocery shopping in the next town over and then she took me to the used bookstore after. He called and asked why we'd been gone for three hours and that we had to get home immediately. When we got home he grounded me for a month.

Stephanie and I played a lot of games together. We made up something called Eraser Game. We both collected a lot of erasers. We'd each place something as a bet—lip gloss, a bracelet, a small toy—then we'd each choose an eraser as our player, using our fingers on the edges to flip them. The first one to flip their eraser and have it land on top of the other's won both the person's item placed for bet and their eraser.

After seeing *Lord of the Rings*, we'd go into the backyard or the woods behind the park and pretend we were battling orcs. When we tired of that, we'd take Daisy, Bill's dog, to the park after we finished cleaning and played Wonder Dog, which was basically Hot Lava Monster but you could only travel if you had Wonder Dog escort you. We'd run home right before Bill got back from work.

I loved Daisy. She unofficially became my dog. I'd sit with her in my bed and tell her all my secrets. What was going on in the sixth grade, boys I liked, girls I didn't like, and how much I hated Bill.

Going through puberty was the worst. Especially when Bill would call my boobs "mosquito bites." After I convinced my mom to start buying me tampons instead of pads, he asked me if putting tampons in felt good.

Another inappropriate thing he said: every year the senior class decorated raglan tees with some fun moniker on the back. I was brainstorming and thought of Dianasauras. He said people would call me Diana Sore-Ass.

This thing would happen where Bill would be eating steak, which my mom cooked a lot because it was his favorite, and it'd get stuck in his throat and he'd start choking. First, he would down his glass of milk to try to wash it down. Then he'd lock himself in the bathroom until he threw it up. Sometimes he didn't make it in time and just threw up all over his dinner plate and made my mom clean it up.

His doctor didn't know why it was happening, but red meat seemed to be the cause and he needed to cut it out of his diet, but he refused to. My mom told him he shouldn't run to the bathroom because what if he was out at a restaurant and nobody knew and he just choked to death? I secretly hoped that would happen. I wanted him to die.

One morning he vomited on the stairs. He told me to clean it up, and then he left for work.

Hanging out with friends was hard. Working up the courage to ask him if we could go was the hardest part. Sometimes he'd say yes, most of the time he'd say no, other times he just wouldn't respond and we'd retreat back to our rooms, too afraid to ask again.

Sometimes our friends were allowed to come over. Stephanie and I each had a friend over one day and he called for us to come to the pantry. He started yelling at us because we ate all the canned mandarin oranges. Stephanie's friend got so scared she called her mom and got picked up immediately. This happened a few times. Eventually, people stopped wanting to come over and I stopped inviting them. Then when I would ask to sleep over at someone's house he'd say no, why don't your friends ever come over here?

I had a pink translucent Game Boy Advance my mom had bought me a few years back. I owned one game: *Britney Spears Dance Beat*. It was sitting on the end table next to the couch and Bill suddenly got mad about something, not even at me, and he grabbed it and threw it across the floor, breaking it. He didn't apologize or buy me a new one.

My mom would often sit at the kitchen table with one leg propped up on the chair by her chest, an Asian habit I've also picked up. He made fun of her and called her Viet Cong.

When my aunt and grandma came to visit us from San Jose, they could sense that something was wrong. We told them everything that had been happening. About a week after they left, Stephanie and I heard a knock at the door as we were getting ready for school. It was my aunt and my older brother. They'd driven up from San Jose to rescue us. They told us to pack our things and that they were taking us back to California to live with them. I was relieved but scared of what would happen when my mom and Bill found out and what he would do to us if we ever had to go back.

We lived in San Jose for two months. My aunt enrolled us in school (me in eighth grade and Stephanie in fifth grade) and started the process of trying to become our guardian. We had to go to court in San Jose. I didn't really understand what was happening. After the court hearing, they put me and Stephanie in a car without telling us anything and we didn't know where we were going, but when they dropped us off at the airport we knew they were making us go home. I say we ran away, but I guess the way my mom saw it, my aunt and my brother kidnapped us. All the legal fees put my mom twenty-thousand dollars deeper in debt.

The first day we were supposed to go back to school, my mom dropped me and Stephanie off at her friend Chi's house for some reason. I think because she had to leave early for work and she wanted someone to keep an eye on us in case we made a run for it again. My brother instructed us to go to the police and ask for help so he had his friend pick us up outside Chi's house and drive us to the police station. I had tickets to a

Green Day concert that night and I knew that by going to the police there was no way I was gonna get to go.

We spent all day talking to different officers, telling our story over and over again. They kept asking us if he ever hit us or our mom and we said no. The possibility of being put in a foster home was brought up at one point, but they said we would have to be separated and that scared us. They transferred us to a different police station and then my mom and Bill showed up and took us home. Because he didn't hit us, nobody could help.

After we got back, Stephanie and I refused to be separated. We stayed in her room for a week, leaving only to go to the bathroom or to sneak food back into the room. We didn't unpack our suitcases from San Jose and would unlock and lock them every time we had to get something out. My mom and Bill demanded that we open them and show them what was inside but we stood our ground. It was the last, tiny, pointless thing we had any control over. They called the cops. It was a power move, but they painted it like we could have been hiding something dangerous or maybe they really were scared we were plotting to kill them. The police officers made us open the suitcases which were just filled with clothes and trinkets. I could tell they were annoyed. This was not the first or last time they'd be called to our house.

A family therapist had to come to our house after the runaway incident. We all sat in the living room and it was really uncomfortable. We only did that once, but it was decided that I had to continue counseling on my own because I was troubled.

My counselor's name was Dan. We talked about books and movies and music. I continued to see Dan on and off from eighth grade through senior year of high school. Once when I was waiting for my mom to drive me to counseling, Bill said that I must be retarded because only retarded people needed therapy.

Dan and I never really got into the deep stuff. Or if we did, we didn't stay there for too long. He never pried. I guess maybe I was wasting my time in counseling, but it felt nice to talk to someone outside my world. He would do this thing where as he was listening, he'd run his finger around and around the rim of his coffee mug. I remember it making me feel slightly uncomfortable. Like it was a pervy thing to do.

We were trying to survive in any way that we could. I stopped talking back and trying to run away. I kept my head down, I kept quiet, I kissed his ass during his manic periods. I was just trying to make it through high school.

Even on my best behavior I still found myself in trouble. One night he was mad at me for something and sent me to bed without dinner. I'd signed up for my own Netflix account with my aunt's credit card. That week it was *Almost Famous*. I popped it in my tiny portable DVD player and propped it up on a metal folding chair. *Listen to Tommy with a candle burning and you will see your entire future.* I saw a way out of my suburban prison, a job I could have ("The Enemy," a rock writer), and I cried and cried.

His fits came on fast. Unexpected and expected. After dinner one night, he marched to the fridge and started dumping every condiment we had on the kitchen floor. Globs of ketchup and mustard and mayonnaise and A1 steak sauce. When he was satisfied he told my mom to clean it up and went to bed. The next morning he yelled at me and Stephanie and asked why there was mustard on the ceiling. We said he did it the night before. He didn't believe us. Either he was so blackout drunk he couldn't remember or he was lying.

When he wanted to hurt my mom he'd call her fat, ugly, disgusting, stupid, and a gook. And that she was lucky she had him because no one else would want such a disgusting woman.

After a particularly bad night, Stephanie and I were huddled in my bedroom. My mom came downstairs and told us she was leaving him and she would call a lawyer the next day. I fantasized about living in a small two-bedroom apartment with my mom, Stephanie, and Andrea. But I didn't get too excited. She'd said it before. The next day, I searched her face and I knew she wasn't doing it.

I still wish she would find the strength to leave him. She has told Andrea that she was staying with him because of her and would divorce him once she graduated from high school. She always made it out like she was doing this for us. But she did this *to* us. I don't think she'll leave him. And if she ever did, I'm scared of what he'd do to her.

I had three boyfriends throughout high school. Boyfriend #1 came over one morning to hang out while I got ready for school because we had late-start or something. I was in my pajamas brushing my teeth. Afterward, Bill told me I should never brush my teeth in front of my boyfriend because it wasn't attractive. Now that I had a boyfriend, I should always look hot for him. After he met Boyfriend #2, he yelled "My daughter is not a slut!" as we left the house. Senior year I was on my way out to meet Boyfriend #3 and Bill wouldn't let me leave the house unless I changed out of a skirt.

I was cleaning up after dinner and he was in front of the TV on his recliner. He told me to go into the bathroom in his and my mom's room and bring out the scale. He made me stand on it. 117 pounds. He called me fat.

Bill didn't have any friends. Aside from the people he drank with at Bert's Tavern. When my mom would tell us that he'd called and said he was at Bert's, we knew he'd come home in a bad mood. His family was just as dysfunctional as he was. He thought he was better than them, so he was always going back and forth between not talking to them and trying to help them. My mom and my sisters were all he had. And he terrorized us because he knew we couldn't leave.

I plotted ways to get back at him. I had a running fantasy of putting peanut butter in his shoes. I never did it. I got really into watching *CSI: Crime Scene Investigation*. I played out in my mind the moments after I killed him. Would I call the cops and say it was self-defense? Could I do it without a trace? Was I so insignificant that no one would think to look for me? Would anyone blame me? But then I remembered the police station. He didn't hit us, so there was nothing they could do.

There were times when we'd get along. I was getting into a lot of the classic rock and heavy metal music that he enjoyed in his teenage years. We even went to see AC/DC and Guns N' Roses together. For a while there I was his favorite. And Stephanie was my mom's favorite. Just like with my dad. I found myself wanting to align with Bill. Wanting to impress him. I thought if he liked me, he'd go easier on me.

He spent a lot of his time in front of the TV, shouting at us to come whenever he needed something. Sometimes he'd call me up from downstairs just to hand him the remote that was two feet away. Sometimes it was for something worse. Getting punished for something we didn't do. We were expected to jump up and run to him immediately. When either Stephanie and I had to shower, we would ask the other person to cover for us and then spend the whole shower trying to listen for

our name. I was too scared to ever even take naps in
case he'd call for me.

For a period of time while I was in high school, Bill
got a job doing long-haul truck driving. He'd be gone
for weeks or months at a time. Those were the most
peaceful moments out of the seven years I lived in
that house. We spoke freely, we stopped holding our
breath, and my mom would cook Vietnamese food[8]
again. But then he'd come home for weeks or a month
at a time. And him sitting at home every day in front
of the TV without the structure of a day job was much,
much worse.

Harry Potter and the Deathly Hallows: Part 2 was playing
at the drive-in and my friend Emily invited me to go
with her. The movie started at dusk—it was summer,
so around 9pm. She came over to pick me up at seven
so we could buy snacks and find a good parking spot.
Bill asked why we were going so early if the movie
didn't start until dusk and were we meeting boys? He
wouldn't let us leave and said we had to sit in the living
room until it got dark. He dozed off at one point and
we snuck away. We were only in the Albertsons for a
few minutes before he called. How dare I disobey him

8
Da Ua

When I would spend
summers with my grand-
ma as a kid, she always
made us Vietnamese
yogurt that she'd put
in baby food jars and
freeze. It was the perfect
summer snack. My mom
recently told me how to
make it.

Pour a can of sweetened
condensed milk in a big
bowl and use that empty
can to fill with boiling
water. Add to bowl and
mix well. Then add 2
can's worth of cold milk
and mix it. Add a can's
worth of plain yogurt.
Mix all together. Pour the
mixed milk liquid over
the strainer—it makes the
yogurt texture smooth.

Divide into small
jars and close the lids.
Heat the oven at 350F
and turn off after about
10 minutes. Put all yogurt
jars in the oven, cover
with some towels to keep
it warmer for around 10
hours. Take all yogurt jars
out of the oven and keep
them in the refrigerator
or freezer. Enjoy!

and I better come home immediately. So Emily drove me back. By this point, she knew what the deal was.

I only applied to two colleges: Western Washington University and the University of Washington. With an 1170 SAT score and listing blogging as one of my extracurricular activities, UW seemed like a long shot. I got accepted to Western for early decision in January. My boyfriend, Dylan, was hoping to get into Western too, so we went to visit the campus with his mom. When I got home that night, Bill asked me what I thought of the school. I told him it was beautiful and I liked it. He asked if I was gonna go there. I said I didn't think I'd get into UW, so probably. He got angry and said that no daughter of his was gonna go to Western. I told him that made no sense and that it was a good school and he didn't even go to college. It escalated and he told me to get out of his house. So I ran downstairs and started packing a bag. Bill called me back upstairs and said he decided I could stay. I said fuck that and I drove to Dylan's where his parents let me stay the night. The next day at school I called my friend Katee during lunch. I told her what happened and asked if I could crash at her place.

Katee lived in a small two-bedroom apartment with her dad and older brother. Katee and her dad each had a room and her brother slept in the living room. It was cramped but they welcomed me with love and understanding. We made a bed for me out of spare blankets on the floor right next to Katee's bed. I stayed with her and her family for three weeks before my mom convinced me to come back home.

That March I stopped at Bartell Drugs on my way home from school to buy Ranch Corn Nuts. I got a call from Bill before I could even check out. Get home now, he said. I asked why and he told me to just do it. When I got home I braced myself for whatever I was in trouble for this time. He handed me a small purple University of Washington envelope that had "The big envelope" written across the front.

A few weeks later, I was at the kitchen counter having an after school snack. Chef Boyardee ravioli. Bill said something about having to do what he says because he was my dad. It made my blood boil. So I said what I knew would make his blood boil: you're not my real dad. That really set him off. He got up from his recliner and his drink, and grabbed the food I was eating away from me. He told me to get out of his house. I was being kicked out again. My car keys that I kept on a purple UW lanyard were on the counter next to me. And just like if we were in a movie, both our eyes darted over to the keys at the same time and we grabbed for them. I don't know how long the struggle lasted, probably a few minutes. We were both tugging on the lanyard trying to wrestle the keys away from the other person. He shoved me and had me pinned down on the ground at one point. My mom jumped on him to try to get him off of me. I had to bite his arm and kick him, but I eventually got away from him. With the keys.

I ran down the stairs as he was still yelling and I started packing. This time it felt different, it felt final. My mom was sitting at the top of the stairs calling the police. I heard a loud tumble and her screaming. He had kicked her down the stairs. Then I heard the front door slam and a car peel away. He'd grabbed Andrea, who was five, and drove away with her.[9]

9
I read the police report. When Bill was pulled over he wasn't wearing shoes and didn't have his wallet. And Andrea wasn't wearing a seatbelt. He called me "crazy." He admitted that he'd been drinking (one screwdriver) and that he was trying to "elude" police because "these situations never work out for males."

A couple officers arrived at the house to take our statements and photos of our scratches and bruises. It didn't take them long to deduce that he was the primary aggressor. He was arrested for two counts of Assault 4 Domestic Violence.[10] They said he'd spend the weekend in jail.

> My mom and I sat at the kitchen counter after the officers left. I asked her what she was going to do and was she going to leave him? She said no. I told her there was no way I was going to be there when he got back. She said okay and asked me to at least spend the night at home and I could leave the next day. So I called Katee and told her what happened. She said oh my god and of course I could come back and stay.

On Monday, I was at school during lunch when I got a call from the sheriff's office. I found an empty hallway to take the call. They told me they were set to let him go and did I want to press charges? I thought about my mom and Andrea. I knew he was a bad man and that we'd all be better off without him, but I was afraid to fracture the family even further. My mom has always told me that she couldn't leave because she needed the financial stability and that she was too old to start over on her own. I thought if I pressed charges I might

---

10

An Assault 4 Domestic Violence charge is made in a situation where two parties have a certain relationship and the individual charged intends to hurt the other party. It requires that the injured party feared actual harm would occur even if there was no physical contact.

In Bill's written statement he said: *Diana and not only with me, has not been getting along w/ our family. She recently ran away for a period of 2 weeks + and I did not know where she was only that I knew she was safe w/ friends. We got into another argument today and she threatened to do it again. I said go ahead but my parental instincts took over and I decided to take her car keys instead so that she could not run away again. In the process of trying to get her keys she bit me and kicked me in the groin area and tore my shirt collar. My wife called the police and jumped on me as I tried to leave the home. I'm afraid of Diana and don't see how she can return to the home w/o help.*

ruin their life in the short-term and they might resent me for it. So I told them no, I don't want to press charges. There I was standing in the school hallway, talking to the cops about pressing charges against my stepdad while everyone else was talking about what colleges they were going to and who they wanted to take to prom.

I was back at Katee's with my bed of blankets. She had to be pulled out of school our junior year of high school because of ongoing, undiagnosed health issues. So I would go to school, work a shift at Cold Stone Creamery and when I got home at night, Katee and I would eat dinosaur chicken nuggets and mango sorbet and watch *Degrassi: The Next Generation*.

Every morning, I'd drive over to the house to pick up Stephanie and drive her to school. I didn't see my mom much during that time. I couldn't go home and Katee's apartment felt cramped enough so there wasn't really room for us to hang out there. Sometimes my mom would drive over and give me a bag of groceries and we'd sit in her car in the parking lot talking for a few minutes. Sometimes she'd bring Andrea, which was the only time I got to see her.

Sharing a small room with Katee got tense at times. She was very active on Tumblr and had a decent following. One day I was reading her blog and she had written about how messy I was and how much it annoyed her. I didn't bring it up with her and I just bought her a soap dispenser shaped like a giraffe, her favorite animal, as a peace offering. It was all very passive-aggressive of us. And driving around with most of my belongings in my car was unsettling. But I was free—sort of. I felt a lot of guilt for getting away knowing that my mom and my sisters still lived in the Monster House. Stephanie and I had always known that because I was three years older, I would graduate and get out first, but we weren't prepared for the way it happened. I tried to remind myself that maybe my leaving would show them that it was possible.

I kind of broke down in Dan's office about how hard it was and how stressed I was about money. He left and came back with two 50-dollar gift cards to Fred Meyer. I was embarrassed to be getting a handout, but I was grateful because I really needed it. I used them to buy food and makeup wipes.

As my freshman year of college approached, I moved out of Katee's. I'd been living with her and her family for five months as I finished high school. My mom arranged for me to rent a room at her friend Carol's house, in the same neighborhood as where my mom, Bill, and my sisters were. When I looked into housing for the school year, the dorms were too expensive and the thought of trying to find off-campus housing near school felt like more stress than I had the bandwidth to take on at the time. And I wanted to stay close to my sisters. So I rented that basement room from Carol and commuted to school by bus.

There were times I was so broke I would buy a big bag of off-brand cereal or a Costco pizza and eat it for every meal for a week. But I didn't care because I had a space of my own and could freely use chopsticks without being ridiculed with racial slurs and finish a bag of chips in the pantry without fear of being yelled at or grounded.

One day Stephanie called me crying. Something had happened and Bill was kicking her out and could I come pick her up? I didn't think twice. I drove the two minutes from Carol's to my mom's and when I got there Bill wouldn't let me through the front door. So I went around the back of the house and crawled through the window to what was now Stephanie's

Bill yelled from upstairs that he was calling the cops.
I told Stephanie I'd wait for her outside by the car. As
I was walking up the stairs to the front door, I could
hear him on the phone with the police. He told them
that his stepdaughter was in his home uninvited and
that he didn't feel safe. My mom met me at the door.
I asked her if she was really going to let him call the
cops on me. She told me that it was his house and he
had a right to.

Stephanie came out and we loaded her things into my
car, parked along the sidewalk. Bill came out on the
lawn and told us the cops were on their way and to get
off his property. I told him I wasn't on his property, I
was on the sidewalk, and that I wasn't leaving until the
cops came.

When they got there it didn't take them very long to
figure out Stephanie and I weren't a threat and told us
we could leave. They told Bill that if they had to come
to our house one more time, they would take him to
jail. So at sixteen, Stephanie came to live at Carol's
with me.

■

It's been twelve whole years since I left home. There's been three houses,
three apartments, and one condo between me and the Monster House.
Every time someone raises their voice or slams a cupboard or I hear heavy
footsteps in the apartment above me, I'm right back in that house. Or when
I'm on the phone with my mom or Andrea and I hear him telling my mom
to speak English or yelling at Andrea for something.

For three years after I left the Monster House, I didn't come home. Not
for Thanksgiving, not for Christmas, not for Mother's Day. Slowly, I started
coming home for those holidays and my mom's and Andrea's birthdays.
My mom would sometimes plead with me to come home more often, to be

okay with Bill. I just want us to be a normal, happy family, she'd say. But I didn't want to be around my abuser.

He doesn't mess with me anymore. Ever since I stood up to him at seventeen, he's scared of me, or maybe he respects me. But I know he still torments my mom and my sister when I'm not around to see it.

I feel guilty that by coming over and acting like everything's okay and even thinking that he's funny and charming sometimes, that I'm enabling this hell of a life they're living. But I know it would kill my mom to lose her daughters again. And I'm so grateful for the relationship I've finally been able to build with her as an adult.

All the advice I hear and read says that you should cut your abuser out of your life at all costs. But doing so would cut my mom and Andrea further off from the people that love them, which is exactly what he wants. My mom is getting older and when she's no longer here, I don't want to regret that I didn't spend as much time with her as I could, because of him. But if something bad happens to her at his hand, I don't want to regret not having done everything I could to get her out, either.

So I'm playing the game. I'm staying close. Until Andrea leaves home. Until my mom leaves him. Which I'm still hopeful she will. As much as I want my mom to leave, I'm scared of what he might do if she did. I want to be around so they know that if they ever needed me, I'd be there.

Andrea's seventeen now, the same age I was when I left. I have my doubts she'll make it until she graduates high school. Which is why I've been working so hard to become stable enough to take her in when the time comes.

Lê Ngọc Anh

■

Fall of Saigon

■

SO THE WAR ENDED IN '75. DO YOU REMEMBER WHERE YOU WERE WHEN THAT HAPPENED?

So the house that we lived in at the time was in a neighborhood of military families. It was its own community and was gated. Before April 30, 1975, that was the start of a lot of ruckus. They wanted to raise the security of the people who lived in this community so they imposed a curfew. The gates would close at 9pm. When entering and leaving you would have to be escorted by a military guard.

We were scared, of course. When the gunfire started, we were afraid our house would get hit. We didn't have a basement to hide in, so we ran to the temple to hide. They had a basement. The entire community hid in there. A number of people ran out to Saigon's big port to be retrieved by the Americans and also to the airport to leave on airplanes to be taken overseas. That final day, the Fall of Saigon, was when a lot of people left. Our family was also supposed to go. The Americans were offering military personnel and their families a chance to evacuate. Because Grandpa was in the Navy, he could have had us evacuated.

WAS THIS IN THE HELICOPTERS?[11]

No, the helicopters flew right into the community where we were living, onto people's rooftops to pick up the highest-ranking military officials. That, I did see. But the people who ran out to the airport, there were US airplanes there to pick them up. All of Grandpa's friends left at that time. They took their wives and their children out to the ports—people were leaving by airplane, by boat. There were a lot of ways and a lot of people. But Grandpa was scared. He was afraid of going over to the United States

DIANA LE

11

This was a question informed by my favorite episode of *Hey Arnold!* where Arnold gets Mr. Hyunh for Secret Santa. He learns that Mr. Hyunh is a Vietnamese immigrant. During the Fall of Saigon, Mr. Hyunh tries to flee with his baby daughter on the last helicopter out of Vietnam. When the pilot announces there's only room left for one more, he offers his daughter. Watching it as a kid, it was the first time I saw Vietnamese people depicted on American television. Even if it was just a cartoon.

and that our family would be unsuccessful because we would be going over with no money.[12] He didn't know how we would live. And there were seven of us kids.

So we didn't go. But the truth is, afterward, there were a lot of people who didn't leave at that time, who weren't sure whether they were making the right decision in staying. The alternative could have been leaving and dying. So Grandpa didn't go. And afterward, Grandpa was put in the camp and the government and society completely changed. So then everyone saw that the decision they had made had been the wrong one.

WHAT WERE YOUR THOUGHTS ON THE WAR AND THE CHANGING GOVERNMENTS? WERE YOU SCARED?

Yes, when the war was nearing our city we were very afraid. Everyone in our extended family who was living farther up north had to flee and stay in our house. Starting in February, we had a few families all living in our house because we were the only ones living in Saigon. They all came to live with us. It wasn't until after the war ended did they return to their villages.

So my teenage years happened after '75, and it was an extremely difficult time. In Vietnam, normally it would be that one income would be enough to feed an entire family. But after '75, Grandpa was detained in a re-education camp. They took everyone who had been in the military.

So Grandma had to go out and try to sell things. She would go out and find things and try to resell them or make tea and try to sell it. She had to go out and sell things to try to feed and raise the children.

SUBURBAN LEGEND

12
One of my cousins told me recently that my grandpa's family was very rich before the war. My grandpa and his siblings inherited different parts of land from their parents. Some of his siblings sold theirs, but he kept his land. After the war ended and North Vietnam took over, they seized the land from him. His siblings who sold their land prior to the war ending remained pretty well off.

■

Eat, But Don't Eat

■

Like the time when I was seven and watching a J.Lo music video and seeing how she had a V-cut going from her hips down toward her vagina. I lifted up my shirt and saw that my seven-year-old girl body had one too. I felt skinny. I felt sexy.

The time in middle school when I watched *Sleepover* and the hot guy saw the main girl for the first time and she was skateboarding in a red cocktail dress. He was like "Who was that?" He looked her up in his old yearbook and the quote underneath her picture said "Hobbies: hot dogs, skateboarding, and napping."

The time I saw *A Cinderella Story*. The scene where Hilary Duff's character is playing 20 Questions with Chad Michael Murray's character and he asks her "Given the choice, would you rather have a rice cake or a Big Mac?" She answers "A Big Mac. But what does that matter?" "Well, I like a girl with a hearty appetite."

The time when I was fifteen and my boyfriend and I went to a music festival and saw Paramore perform. At the end of their set, their lead singer Hayley Williams went off to the side of the stage and scarfed down a cheeseburger. My boyfriend said it was the hottest thing he'd ever seen.

All the times I would make a box of Kraft macaroni and cheese and eat the entire contents straight from the pan. I'd eat past the point of comfort, past the point of fullness, past the point of pain. Then I'd lay in the hallway groaning and feeling accomplished.

The time I was seven and graduated from the Happy Meal to the Big Mac meal and bragged that I could eat a whole Big Mac in less than two minutes.

The time my siblings and I were kids and there was always junk food around. Maybe because we were poor. Maybe because we were raised by a single mother who was always working and just wanted to pacify us.

The time I tried to be anorexic in high school after my stepdad called me fat for being 117 pounds. I skipped breakfast and stopped packing my lunch. After a week I looked in the mirror and I looked gray and ugly so I started eating again.

The time I gained weight my freshman year of college. That summer I visited my family in San Jose and all the aunties couldn't believe how fat I'd gotten. I hadn't even noticed. I got up to at least 125 pounds that year. I stopped checking after that because I didn't want to know.

The time I tried to lose that weight. For lunch, I would just eat a veggie burger patty with ketchup and some baby carrots.

The time I went vegan junior year of college and lost ten pounds in the first month and my boyfriend Dylan commented on how flat my stomach was while we were having sex.

The time I got a new boyfriend, John, and all we did was eat. We made up Pizza Sex Day where we ordered a pizza and stayed inside and ate and watched Netflix and fooled around. And then there was Donut Sex Day.

The time that John broke up with me. I was so sad I lost my appetite for the first time in my life. I just guzzled coffee. I lost ten pounds in three weeks. I probably never ate more than 500 calories a day during that period. Everyone started asking if I'd lost weight and saying how good I looked, even though I was the most miserable I'd ever been. I decided that if I survived this, if I ever got happy again, if I ever got my appetite back, I'd keep the weight off.

The time I started working out three to four times a week. Mostly eighties and nineties workout tapes. Two days on, one day off. I started counting my calories. At first, I was counting to make sure I didn't eat too much. Then I started counting to make sure I was eating enough. As long as I ate at least 1,000 calories, I felt like I would be okay and wouldn't become anorexic or anything. But no more than 1,500 calories. When John and I got back together I told him to let me know if I ever got too skinny because I wanted to be thin but I didn't want to be so thin where it wouldn't be attractive anymore.

The time I went to the doctor and they weighed me and I was 106 pounds. They asked me if I had intentionally lost weight. I told them yes and no. I just started exercising and eating better. I left the office feeling so happy. I'd never weighed so little before.

The time I was obsessed with achieving the measurements of Sir-Mix-a-Lot's perfect woman: 36-24-36. And I did. Except for the boobs.

The time I went to the doctor three years later. The physician's assistant guessed that I couldn't be any more than 100 pounds before I stepped on the scale. I hadn't weighed myself since I'd gone to the doctor the last time, and I still looked just as thin so I just assumed I was still 106 pounds. I weighed 116 pounds. She was really shocked. She tried to make it positive. She said I probably had a lot of muscle. And I knew that was probably true. But I still tried to starve myself for the next few weeks anyway.

I think maybe I'm totally fucked up now.

Like how I've become all of those girls I've always despised and made fun of.

How I have all these rules for myself. Monday–Friday: no fun foods, no more than 25g of sugar a day, no eating out, no alcohol.

How I eat mostly healthy pre-packaged foods so I can read the label and see exactly what's in it and how many calories I'm eating. I don't like cooking at home regularly because I can't tell exactly how many calories I'm eating.

How I started learning how to cook traditional Vietnamese recipes and want to be able to incorporate Vietnamese food into my everyday life but it's a lot of meat and rice and noodles and I'm scared I'll get fat.

How I eat like a robot. I eat the same things every day. Iced coffee with a splash of almond milk.[13] Organic coconut almond chia cereal[14] for breakfast. Half a salad kit with roasted chicken[15] for lunch. Frozen beans and rice burrito[16]

13
20 calories.

14
300 calories.

15
430 calories.

16
260 calories.

for dinner. It's mechanical. Having to think about what I'm going to eat for every meal stresses me out.

How I don't trust healthy recipes or workout routines from anyone who isn't skinny.

How I can't pass a mirror at home without checking my body.

How I'll lift up my shirt and study my stomach to see if I'm still skinny. When my stomach is flat I'm happy. When I look bloated I worry that I'm getting fat. Sometimes I'm rational about it. I think maybe it's because I'm gonna get my period or that I just ate and I'm still digesting. Sometimes I spiral out and think it's definitely because I ate a handful of chips. Then I check my stomach two hours later and it's flat and I'm happy again.

How I hate the inconvenience of having to take a shit but get excited that my stomach might look flatter after I do.

How I'm thin enough where I don't want to lose any more weight. I'm just continually working on getting more toned and making my butt a little bigger. Sometimes I'm jealous of overweight people because they have weight to lose and a tangible goal to work toward.

How I spend all my time thinking about people who can say yes when someone offers them a donut at work. I think about how they must be happier because they know how to enjoy themselves.

How I wish I could go back to before I became so aware of my body. Back before I lost those ten pounds. When I was eating whatever I wanted and never thinking about how my body looked and still feeling attractive and desirable.

How everyone thinks that I must be so happy because I don't have to worry about my weight.

How my weight is all I worry about, actually.

How my counselor asked me what I'm getting out of being this way. She said that Kendall Jenner gets paid to maintain her body. What use is it to me to torture myself?

How I tell her it's because I like the way people look at me. I like complaining that I have to get all my clothes tailored because everything off the rack is too big for me. I like everything I've gained since losing weight. Male attention. Jobs. Friends. Praise. Adoration. Envy. Confidence.

How I also gained fear and insecurity.

How I want to be free from thoughts and worries about my body and food like it was before I lost the weight. I ate whatever I wanted and never thought about my body.

How I want to enjoy myself but I also want to be skinny.

How I guess I don't know which one I want more.

Lê Ngọc Anh

■

Re-education

■

WHEN GRANDPA WAS FIRST SENT TO THE CAMP, HOW DID IT HAPPEN? DID THEY COME INTO THE HOME TO TAKE HIM AWAY?

No, he was called out to a government office along with other military officials. They were told that they would only be gone for ten days. But once they left, they weren't able to come back.

HOW OLD WERE YOU WHEN THIS HAPPENED?

I was thirteen.

AT THIS POINT WERE YOU ABLE TO UNDERSTAND WHAT WAS GOING ON?

Yes, I understood. I knew that he wasn't able to come back. Life at home was very difficult. Your third aunt would go out and retrieve supplies and materials for us to make extra things out of. Things to sew by hand. This way we could sell it to try to make some extra money.

Me and your third and fourth aunts also went out and worked labor jobs. I went to school in the afternoon so I would work in the mornings. I took the bus straight from work to school. It was an extremely difficult time. A lot of the time, there would be one pen that me and your sixth aunt would have to share between us. One person would have to wait at home for the other to finish school so they could use the pen. This was the period after '75.

WAS IT DIFFICULT TO FIND ENOUGH FOOD TO EAT?

Yes, food was difficult. The food was being rationed. The government took over all the food and distribution and all went into a co-op to sell. It was very difficult to sell food in the market. So they would ration it. Every month you could only buy a little meat, a certain amount of rice. It was all rationed, you would only get a certain amount each month. In the time when I had your brother, they cut back on rations so much that even if you had money, you weren't able to buy meat.

HOW LONG WAS GRANDPA DETAINED?

He was there for a few years. He was released and tried to leave to go overseas to America and was caught again. He was captured twice. Once he had escaped, it meant that he couldn't return home. He had to stay at the houses of acquaintances because if he returned home they would know and he would have been captured again.

SUBURBAN LEGEND

DO YOU KNOW HOW HE WAS ABLE TO ESCAPE?

The camp was located in the south. He was able to escape and swim to land. Once there, he was able to take a shuttle back to Saigon. Once he was in Saigon he had to stay hidden and was not able to return home. He would switch off staying at different people's houses. We would only see him if he came to visit at night or if we ran into him on the street. He would pretty much only see Grandma on the street where she was selling things to keep in touch and to see how the kids were doing.

It was another couple of years before he found another way to go overseas. And this time he was successful. Grandpa was in the Navy so he knew how to operate boats. People would pay money to go overseas. But at this time in Vietnam, people had to pay in gold bars. So Grandpa had just paid his fee, and when he got onto the boat, the two people that were supposed to be the captains of the boat were indisposed and were unable to operate the boat. So your Grandpa alone manned the boat the entire way from Vietnam to Thailand. Once in Thailand, he slowly made his way over to America. At this time, Thailand was supporting those who were escaping from Vietnam. The Philippines were also supporting the South Vietnamese. They also had refugee camps. Grandpa came to America in '82 and he's been here since.

SO DURING THIS TIME, WHAT WAS BEING TAUGHT IN THE SCHOOLS?

They were still teaching things like math and science as usual, but we also had a political portion. They were teaching all about communist ways and their history, things that I didn't know up until this point. We were taught about Ho Chi Minh and the Party. They were teaching this to young people like me to show us that South Vietnam had been wrong and communism was right. They were doing this to brainwash the children.

DID THIS UPSET YOU AND YOUR SIBLINGS?

Upset about what?

THE CHANGE IN POLITICS AND THE WAY THAT YOU WERE LIVING. SITTING IN CLASS LISTENING TO THE POLITICAL BRAINWASHING, DID THAT UPSET YOU?

I knew that I didn't like it, but I had to follow it because if you spoke out about it you'd get in trouble. It wouldn't affect just you but your entire family.

DIANA LE

When I told my sister Stephanie about the interview, she asked to sit in. We were doing the interview at Carol's house, where Stephanie and I were both living now. Neither of us knew much about my mom's life before she came to America. Very few Vietnamese American children of immigrants know much about their parents' stories. I suspect this is due to a perceived lack of openness in immigrant parents. This interview was the first time I'd heard any of these stories. And had I not asked, I may have never heard them.

Stephanie asks a question.

STEPHANIE LE: YOU SAID THAT YOU KNEW SOME FRIENDS AND FAMILIES THAT WERE WORKING UNDERCOVER. AFTER THE END OF THE WAR, HOW DID YOU REACT TO FINDING OUT THE TRUTH?

Afterward, everyone was a lot more cautious. We knew that if someone didn't share the same views as us, then we just wouldn't say things to them. I knew a girl that lived very close to our house. There was a year when I was younger, where I had a birthday and Grandpa came home to attend. I didn't dare to tell her that it was my dad, just that he was an older relative. This worked because saying that he was a relative excused the fact that he looked similar. But we couldn't say that it was our dad because we were afraid.

BECAUSE PEOPLE WERE STILL LOOKING FOR GRANDPA?

Yes. We were afraid that if people knew, they would go out and report it to the government. "Oh, we saw this man. Their father is back." When asked, we would say that our dad was being held in a camp. If we knew a person really well, then we didn't have to worry. But otherwise, we had to be extremely careful. We were still acquainted with them, but just in a different way. The personal stuff, we had to hide.

■

Cutest Couple

■

It starts getting chilly so we decide to leave the music festival area and head back to our campsite to grab blankets before the next set. On the shuttle back to the campgrounds, we overhear a couple of drunk girls pondering big questions like "Why can't we live like this forever?" After a few minutes, they concluded, "Because society wouldn't exist." I roll my eyes and smile and squeeze John's hand. The Molly we took was starting to kick in.

By the time we got back to the tent, we'd already decided to ditch the set. John said people warn against having sex on Molly because regular sex won't feel the same. But he said he wasn't worried.

We have sex and say all the things we'd been wanting to say but hadn't. Like how he fell so hard for me, how he couldn't believe everything that had happened in the past four months, and was it okay if he calls me his lady? I tell him how close to him I felt and how I'd be his for as long as he'd have me. And then he says how amazing it is to be with someone who's so passionate, that he can't help but smile when he sees me taking notes and how proud he was to tell everyone I was there on assignment for *Seattle Weekly* and I was hanging out in the media tent.

I thought about those drunk girls. Maybe we *could* live like this forever. John and I. Tucked away in our own little world. Before we told Dylan we were together. Before any of our friends knew we were dating. And just living with youthful abandon and being in secret love or limerence or whatever.

The next day as John and I are walking into the festival, a group of strangers tells us we're the cutest couple at Sasquatch!. And we smile because it wasn't the first time we'd heard that.

Lê Ngọc Anh

∎

College

∎

After high school, if you wanted to get into a certain college, you had to apply. After applying and getting in, you had to test in—and the test was a big test, not just a regular classroom test. For example, let's say a college took 200 people, and 1000 people were tested, they took the top 200 scores and admitted those people.

WHAT DID YOU STUDY IN COLLEGE?

My school was a teacher's school. The school specialized in training teachers. In Vietnam, they had many specialized colleges. Like, your second uncle's school was an engineering school that was separate. It's not together like it is here, like at UW where they house different majors.

SO AS A TEACHER, WERE YOU REQUIRED TO TEACH COMMUNIST POLITICS?

No, not exactly. Once you got into your specialized field of teaching— like your fourth aunt, she also went to the same school that I did, but she graduated before me. She taught botany and sciences. And at that point, I had chosen English Literature because I knew that eventually I would go to America because Grandpa would sponsor us. Because at that time, Grandpa was already in America.

WAS IT JUST GRANDPA OR HAD ANYONE ELSE IN THE FAMILY MADE IT OVER?

No, at that time it was just Grandpa. Grandpa went over in '82. I just remember that the year I entered college, Grandpa was still in Vietnam, he had not left yet. But he was still in hiding. So I had turned in my paperwork to attend that college, but at that time I had just met someone and I was unhappy and did not want to go to college.

When it was near the exam date, you were given a slip of paper that you had to bring with you the day of the exam. Grandpa had asked me if I had gone to pick up my slip yet. I said that I had decided not to take the exam, so I didn't get it. You couldn't take the exam without the slip of paper. So there was only one week left until the exam, and your Grandpa said, "You should just go get it." I've always remembered that. "You should just go get it, and if on that day you don't take the exam, that's okay."

So I went out to get the slip of paper. By the time I received my slip of paper, I had decided that I wanted to take the exam and pass. So I crammed my studying all in that last week. I studied night and day. In the end, I passed the test, was admitted, and attended school there for three years. I finished high school in '80, so I attended college from '81 to '84. When I gave birth to Kha[17] in '84, I had just gotten out of school. When I married your father, I was still in school.

WHEN DID YOU MARRY DAD?
'83. June of '83.

17
My older brother. Kha
is his Vietnamese name.
He chose his Ameri-
can name, Alex, as a
teenager.

■

Sloppy Firsts

■

You were friends with a lot of the guys I'd crushed on and kissed. For someone of my low social standing, boys in the school band like you and your friends were my equivalent of hooking up with someone on the football or basketball team. But you were also in Jazz Band, which is like being on the varsity team.

We talked exactly one time in high school. It was my eighteenth birthday and my friends had surprised me with a box of cupcakes and a bouquet of balloons that I both loved and resented for drawing attention to me all day. I was standing in the band corridor after school waiting for my sister to get out of choir and you walked by and asked me for a cupcake. You said you knew that I didn't know you, but if I gave you a cupcake, you promised to be nice to me. I'd always thought you were cute, so I did.

By our junior year of college, I'd been dating your friend Dylan since our senior year of high school. You and Dylan reconnected and you started hanging around. A lot. By that point, I'd already started having my doubts about my relationship with Dylan. I developed a huge crush on you. Dylan and I'd been together for three years and he'd moved in with me into the basement apartment in our hometown where I'd been living. We were sleeping in separate rooms because he said he couldn't sleep with anyone else in the bed. Despite that, I was starting to feel smothered. And he was kind of tortured and sad, which I felt burdened by.

Back then, when I thought about the differences between you and Dylan, I thought of the scene in *High Fidelity* when Rob asks Charlie why she dumped him for Marco. *"Come on, Charlie, don't hold back, you can say whatever you like."* And her response was *"Marco just seemed to be a bit more... glamorous? You know? More sure of himself. Less hard work. A little...sunnier. Sparkier."* That's how I saw you. I'd find out later that you were just as tortured and sad.

I thought about you constantly. You came over to our place one night to smoke and drink and play *Super Smash Bros.* like we always did and you ended up crashing at our place on the pull-out couch. I fell asleep on the couch across from where you were sleeping. Dylan was asleep in his bed ten feet away. I laid awake most of the night thinking about what would happen if I walked the two steps and crawled into bed with you.

I think Dylan must have suspected my feelings for you because the next time you crashed at our place, he insisted on sleeping with me in my room.

After I moved out of the basement and into off-campus housing, you were a ten-minute walk from my place. I started asking you to hang out on our own.

The first time I asked you to hang out, we watched *Almost Famous*, my favorite movie. I'd mentioned to Dylan we were going to hang out, and he must have suspected something again because he'd driven the twenty miles from his place and showed up unannounced in the middle of the movie to join us.

Then Dylan transferred schools and moved up to Bellingham and he and I continued to date long distance. The plan was for me to move up there once I graduated while he finished his degree.

I kept making plans with you to come over and watch things. We'd sit on your little couch with a foot and a half between us. Even that felt tense. We were watching *The Life Aquatic* and there was a scene where Bill Murray's character leans in to kiss Cate Blanchett's character and gets rejected. I'd thought about leaning in to kiss you the whole movie. But instead of doing that, I asked you if that had ever happened to you.

Of course I felt terrible. That whole year I felt like a piece of shit. It was always the three of us hanging out. Like Lizzie, Miranda, and Gordo. But I had this huge, secret crush on you. I talked about it with my sister a lot. She was basically the only person who knew how I felt about you. And how deeply. She'd known how I was feeling about Dylan way before you even came into the picture. We discussed whether I was actually into you or was I just into you because I wasn't into Dylan anymore and you happened to be in the wrong place at the wrong time for my displaced feelings and attraction?

I used that line of thinking to try to explain away my feelings for you. But I couldn't. I've read or heard that this actually happens a lot with best friends, siblings, and roommates of boyfriends or girlfriends. Because they're enough like your partner to be friends with them—same values, sense of humor, sensibilities, whatever—but they're different enough to offer something that might make them a little more compatible with you.

On Halloween night, I was alone in my room with no plans and I saw that you were on Facebook. So I messaged you. You didn't have plans either. I was hoping you'd suggest that we get together and find something to do, but you didn't. So I asked you for advice on Dylan. I told you I was feeling unsure about our relationship and thinking about breaking up with him. You listened. I secretly hoped that with that information, you would declare your feelings for me. You didn't. But now you knew.

By December, I'd finally found the courage to break up with Dylan. I'd been contemplating it for a long time, but it was hard to figure out if my indifferent feelings toward my relationship with Dylan meant anything or if it was just the natural order of relationships. I had no point of reference. He was my first long-term boyfriend. And it wasn't just about you. I'd had doubts about Dylan for two years, and I'd only known you for one. By the time winter break was over, Dylan and I were done. A few days later, I invited you over to watch *Detroit Rock City*. I announced the breakup as soon as you walked in. But nothing happened that night, really. We laid side-by-side on my twin-size mattress on the floor with our arms touching and watched the movie. It was the closest I'd ever been to you.

The following week, we had plans to watch more movies at your place. You wanted to show me *The Room* and I wanted to show you *The Virgin Suicides*. I'd decided that this was the night. I was going to make a move. I had to find the perfect outfit. I went to two different stores to find the perfect black long-sleeved bodysuit I was looking for, which I wore with skinny jeans. I felt really cute.

We got to the end of both movies and I still hadn't mustered up the courage to make a move. It seemed like you were down to extend the night too, so we put on *Harry Potter and the Chamber of Secrets*. It was 2am by the time it was over and you said you should probably take me home. I sat up, looked at you, and asked, "May I be blunt?" Please do, you said. Then I said it. "Do you want to make out?" That was the first time I'd ever used that move on a guy. You sat up then and crossed your legs. You said it was something we should definitely talk about first. I said I just thought it'd be fun, in my best impression of a cool, nonchalant girl. You thought it would be extremely fun but wanted to know what the implications would be. I said it was just making out, still doing my impression. But you weren't convinced yet. What about the retroactive implications, you asked, because this isn't the first time we've hung out. I said it didn't have to be anything. Besides, Dylan and I were broken up. And then you said what I'd been wanting to hear and hoping you felt: "Well, I have been wanting to make out with you for a while." So have I, I said. You asked me how long. And I told you, "Roughly a year."

And then we kind of leapt at each other. My internal dialogue was screaming. I'M MAKING OUT WITH JOHN! Finally. I couldn't take the will-they-or-won't-they thing anymore.

There was a bag of trail mix on the bed that you attempted to sweep off the bed in one swift motion with your arm like you see in the movies where the dude pushes everything off his desk before hoisting his secretary on it. Only, this wasn't the movies and the trail mix spilled everywhere. We just laughed and kept making out.

I told you that I totally wanted to have sex with you, but I'd rather not that night because I was on my period. So we just kept making out. We made out for what felt like an hour. Only after we finished making out like horny high schoolers did we realize that the M&Ms in the loose trail mix we'd been rolling around in had melted into the comforter.

We finally had sex about two weeks later. You were sweet and generous. You made sure I was comfortable and gave me your full attention. You said you thought we should have sex all the time and I agreed. It felt good to enjoy sex again. But then you started to want to go down on me. I never let guys go down on me. It didn't feel good. At first it would tickle but then it would make my skin crawl. It felt perverted. It reminded me of someone way before you.

We talked about it. I told you about what had happened. You understood but wanted to keep trying. It was how you showed love, you said. Most of the time you asked to, I would say no. But sometimes I'd reluctantly say yes and I'd grit my teeth and lay there waiting until it felt like an appropriate time to tell you to stop. Sometimes I'd lie and say it tickled too much or my clit was too sensitive. Sometimes it would make me so upset I'd cry silently.

I don't know what changed, but after a few years together, I eventually broke open. It started to feel good. It stopped feeling like him. And I started cumming.

Maybe it was exposure therapy. Maybe I just wanted to prove that I could. Maybe it was that I finally let myself trust you. Maybe you were a safe harbor. Maybe I'm healed. Maybe.

We've been together seven years now, including the two months we were broken up while you sampled another life, another girl. In the end, you're still the only boy who's made me cum. Something I never thought I'd feel safe enough to experience.

You were tall and cute in a very clean, cookie-cutter way. You looked nice. And I needed nice. John, my boyfriend of two years, had just dumped me for another girl a few weeks before I met you. After it happened I was dazed and completely crazy. I spent a lot of time wondering if I'd totally misread the last two years. I was constantly internet stalking the girl he left me for. Seeing her post a photo in bed wearing one of his shirts. Seeing them on a road trip together. I couldn't eat. I lost ten pounds in three weeks. And I was really horny all the time. To the point where it physically hurt. But I couldn't make myself cum. Every time I tried, I'd get close and my body would betray me. Like someone pulled the emergency brake and I'd just start sobbing.

So I decided to make a Tinder profile. You had a photo of yourself taken in a gray suit and a turquoise tie holding a microphone, probably taken as you gave a best man speech. I thought wedding party dating profile photos were pretty corny, but I just pretended it was a photo of you doing a stand-up set.

We had one interest in common: a local Seattle band called Dude York. So I messaged you and used that as my opening and asked you out for a drink. You said how about Wednesday, 8pm at Hazlewood? I liked that you were decisive.

The day of our date, I brought an outfit to change into after work. A gray trapeze dress, black tights, and black heeled booties. Something I'd never wear now. Now, I'd make it look more effortless.

After our drink at Hazlewood, you suggested we go get another drink at a bar around the corner. I'd always been the one doing the initiating, the asking, the planning. I liked that you knew where to take me.

You offered to drive me home. When we pulled up at my building and you put the car in park, I asked you if you wanted to make out. So we did. Then I asked you if you wanted to come in. We went through a few condoms trying to get it on, but you kept losing your erection every time. I just needed a fuck so I told you to put it in me anyway. I had an IUD so I wasn't scared of getting pregnant. I just hoped you were clean. I was used to danger. But it was never up to me. Always thrust upon me. This time, I walked right toward the danger, legs wide open.

We saw each other for a few weeks and we continued to have sex without a condom. You came over one day to watch *500 Days of Summer* and a bunch of other movies. Then I got a text from John while we were hanging out. I couldn't stop thinking about it. I didn't say anything to you. I was annoyed that he was ruining our date.

The last time I saw you was at brunch with my friend Grady, who lived upstairs from me. I'd invited him to come because I wanted a second opinion on you. While you were in the bathroom, Grady and I agreed that you were cute and nice but there was something a little off and vanilla about you. We were originally supposed to hang out after brunch, but I told you I had something to do. The something I had to do was meet John for coffee.

It was pretty clear that John and I were probably getting back together, so a few days later, I texted you to end things. I told you you were great but that I was feeling overwhelmed post-breakup and needed to work some things out and that I didn't want to string you along and be "the Summer to your Tom." You liked the reference and took it pretty well. Like Tom, I think you were hopeful that I'd change my mind. You were so normal, so nice. I wanted so bad to want you.

The First Time I Honored My Feelings

You were hands down the hottest boy working with us at Suzzallo Library on campus. You weren't just library-hot either, you were *hot* hot. You listened to the Jam. And we happened to both be watching *The X-Files*. So I Facebook messaged you about it and we quickly came up with a hypothetical drinking game to accompany the show.

Me: every time mulder leaves a message on Scully's answering machine

You: anytime they get bitched at by the higher-ups

Me: whenever Scully just misses a paranormal event

You: i feel like this list is comprehensive enough to get drunk after one episode

Me: hazard of believing

You: alright, one more. Every time Scully gives Mulder that look a mix of attraction and annoyance i can't describe it, but i feel like you know what i mean

Me: Every time it's aliens

You: hold on that's not fair at all that's literally every episodes

*episode

Me: No it isn't!

Sometimes it's bees

This was around the same time I started hooking up with John. Things with John were super casual at that point, we weren't exclusive yet and I wasn't sure if anything would come of it. So I kept up my flirtation with you. I invited you to see this band Cumulus with another girl we worked with at the library. It happened to work out exactly as I'd hoped and she got sick so it would just be me and you. I wore a high-waisted mini skirt, a black American Apparel bodysuit that was cut really low in the back, black over-the-knee socks, and chunky black oxfords. You told me I looked great.

We got drinks at the bar while the opening bands played and it felt very grown-up. We stood in the audience when Cumulus came on and you kept putting your arm around my waist. Which was cute but made it hard to dance. I took you back to my place after and I asked you if you wanted to make out, the same move I'd made on John a week before. It was becoming my signature move. We got close to having sex but it wasn't really working. I don't remember why. Maybe you couldn't get hard or something. You apologized and told me it had been a while and you hadn't done it since you and your ex broke up.

At work we'd text and flirt and I even threw out the idea of making out in the basement during your shift down there, but I was starting to catch feelings for John, so I chickened out.

We were walking home together one night after a closing shift and you asked me if I wanted to go to Aladdin for gyros and fries. I went home with you after that and we put on *Spinal Tap*. You asked me if I wanted to make out, using my own move on me. And I hesitated. I told you that I did but that I was kind of hanging out with someone else and I think I might really like them so I didn't think I should and that I was sorry. Even in the moment, I couldn't believe I was turning you down. You were so hot. I knew the other girls at the library would've killed to be in my position. But I couldn't ignore the chemistry I had with John. And you surprised me again. You said it was okay and you insisted on walking me home.

I met you in an acting class I was required to take for my film major. You were a Computer Science major. I always wondered why you were in that class but never asked.

We'd been flirting here and there, but when we got paired up as scene partners for our final project, I knew it was on.

Our scene was from *The Heidi Chronicles* by Wendy Wasserstein. In the scene, Heidi's at a dance and meets this guy named Scoop. And after some witty banter, the scene ends with them kissing. I thought it was weird that our section leader didn't mention anything about it when he assigned it to us. I wondered if we were really supposed to kiss in front of the class or if it was left in by mistake.

I went over to your house one night so we could rehearse. We ran lines in the basement a handful of times and every time we'd get to the end where the kiss happens, we'd say "and then we kiss" and run it again.

After running the scene four or five times, we finally kiss when we're supposed to. We kiss longer than we needed to.

You invite me up to your room and we watch the first twenty minutes of *An American Werewolf in London* before we start making out again.

Later that week, I invite you to a pre-screening of the new Nicholas Holt zombie movie but we got there too late and the theater was full so we got milkshakes instead. After milkshakes, we went back to my room and made out again. We were laying there cuddling and you asked if I was glad you came over. I thought I was playing it cool or casual or something so I said, "I guess so," which was pretty mean and I felt bad about it immediately and I could tell that maybe your feelings were hurt, but I didn't apologize. I don't know why.

We performed the scene for our final on the last day of class (no kiss) and things just fizzled out after that. I always thought that if we had worked out, we'd have had the perfect meet-cute.

THE FIRST TIME I FELT COMPLETELY UNDESIRABLE

I was twenty, a junior in college, and you were twenty-nine. You were a regular at the mail shop I was working at. You worked down the street at this little company called Indieflix that was basically Netflix but for indie movies. Your company had an account with us, so you always came in around 1pm to pick up the mail. Since I was studying film, I tried talking movies with you. I started looking forward to you coming into the shop every day.

One day in the shop, you told me you were going to a screening of *Samsara* at the Cinerama and maybe I should come. I asked a friend to come with me and when we walked into the theater I saw you sitting with your friends. One of your friends hit you on the arm and pointed at me like is that her? I half smiled and waved and my friend and I sat down a few rows away. I sat through the whole movie with my skin prickling, thinking of you sitting elsewhere in the theater and wondering if you were looking over at me.

After the movie, my friend and I walked outside and you and your friends were out there talking. Were you waiting for me to come out? We all hung out in front of the theater for a bit talking and I felt awkward because your friends were all asking me about school and they were all so much older and I wondered if they were secretly judging you for being into a college girl.

We started hanging out alone after that. You told me you had a Cinema Studies degree from UW, the same degree I was working toward. After graduation, you'd moved to LA for a few years and worked as a production assistant. But things didn't really pan out so you'd recently moved back home and were living with your parents. When you finally got your own apartment, you tried to get your parents to pay for your furniture. I wasn't sure how I felt about that. Okay, I did know. Like dude, aren't you an adult? I was disappointed. I thought dating an older guy would be fun and sophisticated. I thought you'd have it figured out and we'd just have amazing sex all the time because you'd be so much more experienced. But none of that was the case.

You'd pick me up from my dorm-size room and ask me how school was. We went and saw a movie at the Metro and you remarked that you hadn't been to this theater in a decade. I thought, a decade ago I was ten.

In the couple of weeks that we saw each other, we only got to third base. Every time we'd hook up, I'd try to initiate sex, but you always pushed my hand away or pulled me off of you and we'd just keep making out. But I kept trying. You finally said something. You said you thought we should wait. I asked for what and for how long? You didn't know, you just wanted to wait longer. I don't know if you felt weird about the age difference or if you just weren't as experienced as I thought you were or something, but I stopped seeing you after that.

We finally got together in our senior year of high school. I'd spent all of junior year flirting with and hooking up with random guys just to distract me from my failed attempts at trying to make you fall in love with me. I tried Facebook messaging you. Multiple times. And you'd barely respond. I grabbed your phone from you while we were standing in the hallway between classes and saved my number in your phone. I spent months and months working on a mixtape for you.

I decided Valentine's Day would be the day I'd give it to you. I was obsessed with grand gestures. I knew you had chemistry with Mr. Sevald third period because my friend McKenzie was in that class. I wrapped the mixtape in blue *Rugrats* wrapping paper with a red bow, snuck into the classroom before you got there, and placed it on your desk then went to my third period class, US History with Mr. Kink. McKenzie texted me during class to tell me what happened. You'd walked to your desk, picked up the tape, and said "What is this?" When you saw that it was from me, you walked half the length of the classroom to the garbage can and threw it away. You met my grand gesture with a rejection just as grand. I was completely embarrassed. Mostly because I knew that everyone who'd been in your class when I delivered the tape knew what happened.

I waited while you hopelessly crushed on another Asian girl and then dated a different Asian girl before finally dating me our senior year of high school. There were definitely times during our relationship where I wondered if you had an Asian fetish or something.

It took us a long time to finally have sex. Was I your first? I can't remember if you'd had sex with the Asian girl before me. You couldn't stay hard enough for us to do it. We tried for what felt like weeks. I think you must have been nervous or something. I suggested we try doing it from behind because maybe you'd be less nervous if you didn't have to look at me. When we finally got the hang of it, we had sex a lot. In your bed, on the hood of your car in front of your parents' house late at night, at the house where my friend and I were house-sitting, where we had sex six times in one day.

Two years into our relationship, I started to feel things shift. I started thinking about breaking up with you all the time. I wished you'd do something like cheat on me so I'd have a reason to. I started loving you more like a friend or a brother. But you were my first long-term relationship, so I thought that might be what was supposed to happen. So I stayed, stayed, stayed.

Even my body knew before I did. My vagina got so tight and dry that every time we had sex it became super painful. You'd initiate sex over and over again and I'd say no, I was tired, or I didn't feel like it until saying no became exhausting and I'd say okay and we'd pull out the lube. Sometimes I'd lay there lifeless. One time I started crying. I don't think you even noticed. I was just waiting for it to be over.

Around our three-year mark, I told you I wanted to go on a break. I wanted to experience being single in college, if those really were our prime years. You agreed but didn't handle it very well. You were very needy and would guilt me into hanging out and every time we did, you asked if we could be back together yet.

Dealing with all that guilt became exhausting and I'd made out with a few boys and thought maybe that was enough, so I said yes, we can get back together. And that's when you started hanging out with John again. And when I started falling for him.

A year later, I broke up with you. For good this time. It was the start of winter break, and you'd come down to Seattle from Bellingham to spend it with me. When you got there, I told you I wanted to break up. You asked if we could stay together at least until winter break was over. I didn't know if you thought maybe you could change my mind during that time, but I felt bad that you'd come all the way down, so I said okay. We spent three weeks eating junk food, watching TV, and cuddling.

When it was time for you to go, I was sadder than I thought I'd be. You were my best friend. We hugged by your car for a long time and then you drove away.

Sometime after we broke up but were still friendly, before John told you that he was dating me and you told him that he broke your heart, you told me that one day you hoped that I'd tell you why we broke up, really. Once in a while, I remember this request and wonder if I owe it to you, if you still even want to know. I thought about writing you a letter but never did.

I found the breakup speech I'd written hoping it would help me figure out what to say to you. It was all about how I felt I'd lost myself in my relationships and how the only time I'd ever really been single was my junior year of high school and how much I grew that year and how I missed that feeling and that girl. I said that we were young and at a pivotal age and should be focusing on ourselves. And how I was overly empathetic to the people around me and I couldn't figure out what parts of me were mine and what parts I just took from the people around me. I wanted to step away and strengthen my beliefs and my feelings and my interests. That in the past year I'd done some growing and had started to break out but that I'd hit a plateau and I couldn't continue growing unless I leave and do it on my own.

All of these things were true. But I can see how it sounds like a bullshit non-breakup. Yes, I'd fallen in love with your friend. But even before that, my feelings for you had curdled and turned into resentment. I found your lack of self-sufficiency and your dependence on me unattractive. Sometimes it felt like you were holding me hostage. We once got into a fight and I left to cool off in my room. When I came back, you had a welt on your forehead the size of a golf ball because you'd been banging your head against the wall until I came back.

I wanted to be a writer and have a career. You wrote poetry and were doing a degree in graphic design, but you didn't want to work. I was ambitious and felt burdened by the thought of carrying both of us. I imagined our life together, me working to support you and your art. I didn't want that.

I hope this answers your question.

The First Time I Acted Like It Didn't Bother Me

You were popular and on the baseball team and had a nice butt and were kind of goofy and obnoxious in a cute way. You said that if we hooked up, we had to keep it on the DL because there was this other girl you liked and you didn't want it to get back to her. I said that was perfect because I liked another guy and I didn't want it to get back to him either. But I did wonder if you just didn't want it to get out because you were embarrassed of me or something.

Right before you came over, I texted my friend saying that I was about to go where many women have gone before.

My evil stepfascist had gone to bed and forgot to close the garage door, so I snuck you in through the garage instead of through my window like I normally would. We started making out on my bedroom floor. You asked if we needed to use a condom and I said um, yeah. So you put one on and we had sex on the floor for like two minutes before you came.

A year later you texted me wanting to hook up again. I told you I was dating that guy that I liked now and you said "That's awesome."

The First Time I Tried to Laugh It Off

I'd been texting this guy Mark and he invited me over to someone's house one night to hang out. He and a few others came to pick me up and I snuck out my bedroom window to meet them. When we got to the house, Mark went off somewhere upstairs and I ended up on the couch next to you.

I'd never been attracted to you. You weren't my type at all. You were small and goofy looking. But I made out with you on the couch anyway. I don't know why. I even let you finger me under the throw blanket. It didn't feel good and it didn't feel bad. But I thought this is what high schoolers did. Living with youthful abandon and letting random guys they didn't like finger them. Then someone walked in and was like "Didn't she come here with Mark?" And I felt called out and didn't know what to say so I think I just laughed it off. Then for a few days after, you were texting me and I was kind of blowing you off and then later that week I was walking to my car in the school parking lot and I heard someone yell "Slut!" and I knew it was you.

The First Time I Was Scared I Was Becoming My Mother

I lost my virginity to you. We didn't have anything in common. You lived in a trailer park with your mom who had the same name as me. You wanted to be a welder after high school. My family was working class, but I didn't think I wanted to stay working class, so I was conflicted about my future with you.

Your dad was in jail or prison or whatever because your sister had come forward about him molesting her as a kid. You were really angry with her but I told you that I believed her.

My bedroom was in the basement, and after my parents were asleep, I'd text you to come over. Sometimes you'd ride your bike over or steal your dad's truck and drive it without a license and I'd sneak you in through my bedroom window. We did this for a while where you'd come over, we'd make out or do other stuff and you'd go home or sometimes stay the night and sneak out early in the morning. One night, I told you I was ready. You immediately got up and ran to the 7-Eleven a mile away to buy a condom. I was surprised that it didn't hurt like I'd always heard your first time would.

I kept my padded bra on the whole time because my boobs are small and I thought that'd be sexier or something.

You called me one night while you were tripping on shrooms at a house party and you'd locked yourself in the bathroom and couldn't get out because the door handle kept changing shapes. Sometimes you'd disappear for days, no calls, no texts, and your phone would be dead and I'd be so worried and over it but then you'd reappear and everything would be okay until the next time.

One time we were laying in bed talking and you said that if we ever broke up for some reason that I should call you after I graduated and maybe we could try again. I still don't know what made you say that.

We'd been together for eight months. The longest I'd ever been with anyone. I sat you down one day in one of those seating areas in the mall where husbands sat and waited while their wives shopped and told you that I wanted to go on a break. I don't remember what the reason I told you was. The truth was that I'd started talking to one of my exes, and was confused and thought maybe there was something still there with him. You started crying right there in the mall, which I didn't expect. I felt awful but it also made me feel like maybe you liked me enough that if I changed my mind, you'd agree to take me back.

A couple weeks later, after I'd gone out and hooked up with my ex and felt nothing, I tried to get you back. But you told me you didn't think we should.

I went to the football game and I never went to football games, just to see if you were there and what you were doing. I saw you there with another girl from school.

I thought about what you'd said in bed that day, about how we could try again later. I clung to that hope for longer than I should have.

You're still dating that girl I saw you with at the football game. You guys have a pit bull together and she manages a Domino's and you're a truck driver now, the same job my stepdad had in high school. I can't help but think that I'd escaped my mother's fate.

THE FIRST TIME I FELT LIKE I'D NEVER BE ENOUGH
Sophomore year of high school, you just kind of showed up and became periphery to my friend group. We liked a lot of the same screamo and post-

hardcore music and you'd come out to shows with us. I'd invite you over to watch movies I wanted to introduce you to. Not *The Notebook*, but *Memento* and *The Boondock Saints*.

We were making out on the couch in the basement and you asked me if I trusted you. I said yes and you fingered me. And I started giving you hand jobs.

I was at my friend Jake's house and you came over to watch *Tenacious D in the Pick of Destiny* with us. I think Jake was sitting on the couch or something and we were laying on the living room floor under a blanket and you started fingering me with Jake a few feet away and his mom in the other room. She walked in at one point. And I was so nervous and mortified because I thought maybe Jake and his mom could tell something was going on. But I didn't do or say anything. It felt oddly familiar. But I wouldn't realize why until the fourth draft of this essay.

You broke up with me out of the blue and I started hearing from other girls that you'd been cheating on me. You texted me a week later saying that you'd gone to change your relationship status on Myspace and it'd made you sad and miss me and could you come over? You told me you wanted to get back together. I was so happy. We were back together for two weeks before you broke up with me again. I think you were fucking a girl from your church.

A while later, we started talking again here and there in the hallways at school. It felt nice to fall back into that familiar banter with you. I thought there might still be something there. We went to see *Transformers* together and made out in the movie theater. I think you made it clear that you didn't see us getting back together and you just wanted to hook up. After the movie, we hid behind a mall dumpster and I gave you a half-hearted blow job and finished you off with my hand. I felt nothing.

The First Time I Felt Like a Joke

You were my first kiss. I was a sophomore and you were a freshman. I'd liked you since the first time I saw you when I was in eighth grade and you were in seventh. Even though you were younger, I couldn't believe you would date someone as awkward as I was. You were tall and pale with your hair dyed dark. I told my friends you looked like a really hot vampire so we started calling you Edward.

One time we were making out and you started rubbing the inside of my thigh and my crotch outside my jeans and when we were done, you looked down at your hands and they were dyed blue from the cheap Forever 21 jeans I was wearing. I was too embarrassed to even laugh it off.

We only dated for a month before I got a call from your ex-girlfriend's best friend saying that you'd been cheating on me with your ex the whole time we were together. Then your ex started texting me, saying that she was in Boston visiting her brother and she ended up in the hospital because she had an ovarian cyst and she might die so she'd just wanted to have sex with you one last time and how she also let you titty fuck her. What a psycho.

THE FIRST TIME I WENT NUMB

My first memory of masturbating was when I was three. I leaned up against the corner of yours and mom's bed and humped it. Another time, I was five, and I was in my bed humping my Disney comforter that I'd bunched up into a ball. My door was slightly ajar and you walked by and saw me but didn't say anything.

I remember this one day when I was a kid and I think we had some family and friends over and the adults were all playing cards in the living room on the floor. You were laying horizontal on the couch and I had squished myself behind you, between you and the couch cushions. I remember laying there feeling a weird mix of emotions. Like this affection for you and almost an attraction and pretending I was in a relationship with you. I think Mom said something about me being back there and you told her to let me be. Was she jealous? Did she know?

One morning before kindergarten I was home alone with you and we were laying on the floor of the living room under a blanket and you were rubbing me between my legs. You spread the lips of my little girl vagina and you stuck your fingers inside. Your fingers felt big and rough and calloused. I just lay there silently. I think in the back of my mind I knew it was strange, but you were my dad, you wouldn't do anything to hurt me. I don't remember what happened after that. I assume you pulled my panties back up, I got dressed, and you walked me to school.

This is the only memory I have of this happening. But I figure it probably happened other times because in high school I was driving home one night from my boyfriend's house and I caught an episode of *Loveline* on the radio where this dad called in and he was concerned about his four-year-old daughter because he'd caught her masturbating. Dr. Drew explained that masturbation at such a young age could be tied to sexual abuse.

I felt guilty for years because I didn't stop you, I didn't say anything. I didn't tell Mom until three years later, after you were already dead. Maybe it was my fault because I liked being your favorite, and maybe that somehow meant that I liked it.

I had a hard time with your death. And maybe I was suicidal. I was sent to see the school counselor because I was thinking about death all the time. I had seen a Chinese drama where a woman was being tortured and restrained and she bit her tongue off and committed suicide in defiance. I don't even know if it's possible to kill yourself by biting off your tongue or maybe I misunderstood that whole scene, but I thought about that a lot and would constantly see how hard I could bite my tongue until I chickened out.

I can't handle watching any TV shows or movies that deal with the subject of incest or pedophilia. I wish there was a specific content warning for that type of thing instead of just "strong sexual content." But sometimes I'll watch daddy-daughter or stepdad porn. It feels really fucked up. My counselor says it's my way of reclaiming pleasure and agency in what happened to me.

People always look so guilty and say how sorry they are after they innocently ask me where my dad is and I tell them that you died when I was eight. Sometimes I tell them it's okay. Sometimes I say it's okay, he was a bad man. But really, I want to tell them that I'm glad you're dead, because if you were still alive I'd probably murder you.

Lê Ngọc Anh

■

Jail

■

How did you meet Dad?

Your fourth aunt had gone out to do some paperwork at a government office or the electric company or something, and somehow met your dad. They ended up talking and she asked him about ways to get overseas. If you were talking to someone and you thought you could trust them, then you asked them about getting overseas. Your dad said that he knew someone who could help us. So that's when I started to get to know him.

And Dad was from the North, right?

Yes, he was born in Hanoi. Dad's family was from Hanoi. In 1954,[18] the year Dad was born, his parents took their whole family to South Vietnam to live. That was the year of the biggest battle that split the country into two.

When did you get divorced?

It was only about a year after Kha was born,[19] about '86. So Kha was living with me at Grandma's house. Oftentimes, your dad would come pick Kha up on the weekends to see his other grandmother. So at the end of '88, your dad and your brother went overseas during one of the hardest times. They weren't accepting any boats that were going overseas. Your dad came to pick Kha up to take him overseas, but he hid it from me. Once Monday came around and it was time for me to go to the school to teach, I waited, but they never showed up. I went over to your dad's mother's house, and she told me that he had taken Kha overseas. I waited and waited, and after several months, there was still no news from them. Because if you were successful, you would send a message by letter. And the journey that your dad and brother went on was full of difficulties.[20] There were a lot of bad people who would take advantage of those who were traveling overseas to flee because they would often carry gold with them to trade. So while I waited and didn't hear anything, at home we had found a way for me to go overseas. But we had gotten tricked.

18
Making him eleven years older than my mom.

19
My dad was a heroin addict. My mom told me years after he died that she didn't find out about his drug abuse until after they were married. She was upset with his siblings and his family because they all knew and hadn't told her.

20
My brother would always tell this story about how they had to drink their own urine at one point.

It was all through acquaintances. Your uncle knew someone, who knew someone, who introduced us to someone. They told me to take the shuttle down to the western side—once there, there would be someone to pick us up. At nightfall, we went down to the small boat. Once we got to the boat, they had us write some sort of phrase for our family so they would know that we had made it onto the boat. At home, they were to have the money ready. So once Grandma received that slip of paper with the phrase on it, she handed over the gold. After all the gold was collected from the families, the boat kept running around and around in circles and the engine broke down. So they took it to shore and dropped us off there. They had scammed us. Eventually, they just left us there. They said that they were stopping to wait for the boat to be repaired, but they left us there. Everyone on the boat knew that we'd all been scammed.

You were alone?

Yes, I was alone.

Were you scared?

I was scared, of course I was. I ran to a small island. I still had a small amount of gold. I had to run and hide or else I would be caught. That night I ran and hid in a house. I told the people there how much gold I had, and asked them to take me to the bus station in order for me to return to Saigon. I don't remember what happened, but they let me stay the night. And in the end, no one was willing to do it or something, so I got caught. I was fortunate because there were people who when caught, encountered bad people and were killed. I was put in a jail along with many different types of criminals. The women were allowed to stay with the women. I was held there for three months. They let you write to your family and inform them that you were being held there. They didn't feed you the way that jails do here. Your family had to bring you food so you could eat. Either that or send you money so you could buy food there.

And was this jail far from Saigon?

Yes, it was far. It was a few hours by bus.

What were you thinking throughout this time?

I was scared. And I still didn't know the whereabouts of your brother. I didn't know whether he was alive or dead. Because there were so many boats that were captured and killed. I was still in jail when I finally received the news that he was okay. Your third aunt came to visit me to tell me the news.

When I was released, I had to pay a fine. Back then, the Vietnamese government would take your money any way they could. Grandma and your third aunt had to pay a certain amount of money. For anyone who didn't have the money, they'd be forced to stay there for however many years to make up for it.

When I got back, I did not return to teaching. That year that I got back, it was '90 or '91, the US was accepting immigrants again. Grandpa had prepared sponsorship papers before then, but they had discontinued all services.

At this time, your dad and brother were already in the US, and so was Uncle Ve. On the sponsorship forms, family members who were already in the US had to first collect their spouses and their single children. Your seventh aunt was the only one who was unmarried, and I was divorced at the time, so she, Grandma, and I all got to go first. After that, Grandpa would continue to slowly sponsor the rest of the family over.

■

Someone Else

■

WHEN I OPEN the door, John is already crying. Or maybe he was still crying from when he called earlier. We sit down on my couch and he starts talking. I don't remember exactly what he said and in what order. But I knew he was breaking up with me. It was like in TV and movies when the main character is getting bad news from the doctor and the camera pushes in on their face and the doctor's voice gets all muffled. You can't hear what they're saying, but you understand anyway.

I hear things in pieces. He feels regretful for giving up music to pursue a career in tech. He thinks money has changed him. Our relationship is comfortable and that makes him sad.

I listen to his list of reasons why we need to break up. I take it all in, and as genuine as it is calculated, say, "I wish you peace and happiness," enunciating the way Rory Gilmore had in the episode where Lorelai accidentally serenades Luke at karaoke with Dolly Parton's "I Will Always Love You." I did want him to find peace and happiness. But I also understood that it was in my best interest to respond to rejection in a classy manner. Kindness is disarming. His face crumples. "You're so kind," he says, and then he hugs me.

I thought about all the cruel things he'd said to me the three other times I could tell he was trying to break up with me over the course of our two-year relationship. He said I had a sad girl aesthetic, that he hung out with me every night because he felt sorry for me, that we had nothing in common. But he chickened out every time I would ask point-blank if we should just call it. Because even then I knew it wasn't worth holding onto someone who couldn't make up their mind about me. Or I at least wanted it to look like I knew that.

"There's something I need to know. Is there...someone else?" I knew the answer. Guys don't break up with their girlfriends unless they have another girl lined up. It just doesn't happen.

"Someone from my past has re-entered my life."

"Is it Anna?"

Anna was the girl he was seeing before we dated. A few weeks before, he'd been sick and we were laying in bed watching TV on his MacBook and these texts popped up on the screen. It was Anna. She said that she was sick too and he shouldn't be surprised if she just came over. I saw the texts but didn't say anything. And neither did he.

"Yes."

"Are you leaving me to be with her?"

"I'm not leaving you to date her. I just don't know what it means about us that this person can shake what we have like this."

I thought about asking if we could have sex one last time. But I remember that he was breaking up with me because there was probably a girl he liked better than me and thought was more attractive. I felt too insecure to ask him if he'd have sex with me, unlike the night I'd first asked him to make out with me. I was afraid of the answer this time.

"Will you lay with me for a bit?" I finally ask instead.

We laid there in limbo for a while, knowing that when we got up, we'd be living in our new realities.

I was already nostalgic for what we had and grieving for what we never would. And I resented that he chose to break up with me on *my* couch, where I would need to spend the next six to nine months wallowing.

Lê Ngọc Anh

■

Coming to America

■

'91.

When you say that the US was accepting immigrants, did this mean that you no longer had to fear being caught?

It means that we were allowed to go. But in Vietnam, you really couldn't feel safe until you actually left the country. We were very scared. We got to go, but we had to be careful. If the government could find any reason to keep you from going—even if it was just because they hated you—they could find even the smallest reason to hold you back. You just didn't have freedom.

What were your first thoughts upon arriving?

I was very happy. I was reunited with your brother. That was before your dad and I got back together,[21] so I lived with your grandma.

How was it to see American houses and neighborhoods?

I thought that they were beautiful and spacious, but truthfully, Grandpa's house at the time wasn't very beautiful or all that spacious. I was confused. I think both your aunt and I were confused. The house was really old. And when we went to other people's houses, they were really big and beautiful.

What did you do first? How long was it before you found work?

When we first came over, and more of our family started coming over—Grandpa's friends were all there too, so they all came to visit us. That initial period that we were there, we always went out to eat and were being

21
This is why there is a seven-year age gap between me and my older brother. My mom and dad divorced in Vietnam after having my brother. And then my dad kidnapped my brother and took him overseas. It was years before my mom would make it to America and reunite with them.

invited to people's houses to eat. We met a lot of people. At first, I went to study cosmetology. I was studying that while I was pregnant with you.[22]

HAD YOU HEARD THAT THE VIETNAMESE HAD FOUND SUCCESS IN COSMETOLOGY?

People had said that if you went to school for that, once you got out you'd make more money. And because at that time I was pregnant with you, I couldn't really go out and ask for work, so I used that time to go to school. A lot of people studied cosmetology, but the number of people who came out and worked in that field was very little.

WERE YOU ABLE TO FIND A JOB IN THAT FIELD?

Yeah, I did a couple of times. But once I started giving birth to you guys, jobs cutting hair became harder to balance because you had to work from ten in the morning to around eight at night. And since I had small children, it wasn't very convenient. So when we moved up here [to Washington State], I started working in factories so I could go to work early in the morning and come home in the afternoon to take care of the family more easily. When you come out of schooling for cosmetology, you don't make a lot of money right away, it takes time. But I needed money right away, so I went to work in a factory so that I could get a secure paycheck and benefits.

DIANA LE

22
I was born in 1992, one year after she arrived in America. My mom and my dad were still technically separated when they had me. He's not even listed on my birth certificate.

■

Pillow Talk

■

SmarterChild: Hi, I'm SmarterChild, a virtual chatterbot meant to give AOL users instant access to news, weather, stock information, movie times, trivia, yellow pages, listings, sports scores, and more! What can I help you with today?

caliv13tgirl: Do you ever talk to your pillow at night?

SmarterChild: Uh...yeah!

caliv13tgirl: I've done it since I was a kid.

SmarterChild: I have fond memories of my childhood.

caliv13tgirl: The first time was with a body pillow that I would pretend was Zach Morris. I would kiss him and pretend he was my boyfriend.

SmarterChild: He wasn't your boyfriend.

caliv13tgirl: I moved on to the regular pillow in my bedroom and would talk to it every night in bed.

SmarterChild: Every night, huh?

caliv13tgirl: I'd pretend my pillow was other celebrities. Like Nick and Brian from The Backstreet Boys.

SmarterChild: Wow...

caliv13tgirl: Sometimes it would be boys from school I liked.

SmarterChild: Care to see today's weather forecast?

caliv13tgirl: I'd play out scenarios. Flirting with them, being courted by them, making out with them. Then we'd become boyfriend and girlfriend.

SmarterChild: Maybe I picked the wrong career.

caliv13tgirl: A lot of times it would be sexual and I'd roll up the corner of my blanket and masturbate.

SmarterChild: If that's what you want, you should play with someone else.

caliv13tgirl: A couple of times it was incestual.

SmarterChild: I don't understand this fully enough to say anything smart about it...

caliv13tgirl: There was a period in the fifth grade where the fantasy was that there was a line of boys outside my bedroom door that would come in and have sex with me one at a time. I'd masturbate over and over to that until I got tired and fell asleep.

SmarterChild: You are not making any sense.

calivi3tgirl: One time when I was really young, like in the second or third grade, my cousin showed me this meme that said "Every time you masturbate, God kills a kitten." I asked him what masturbate meant. He said it was when you have sex with your hand.

SmarterChild: Obsessed with this topic much?

calivi3tgirl: I thought maybe I'd been masturbating wrong because I never used my hands.

SmarterChild: My creators did not give me hands.

calivi3tgirl: Then one day at daycare my friend had just seen *IT* and was telling me all about it. It was horrifying but then I got really really horny. I went into the bathroom of the daycare and laid facedown on the bath mat and tried humping my fist.

SmarterChild: IT is a 1990 two-part miniseries about a predatory monster that has the ability to transform into its prey's worst fears, exploiting the phobias of its victims.

calivi3tgirl: I was too scared to look at real porn, you know with actual people.

SmarterChild: You *real* people sure are strange and complicated.

calivi3tgirl: So I'd scroll through the lewder AOL buddy icons. Like the boobies one and get turned on by that.

SmarterChild: What would you like to know about buddy icons?

calivi3tgirl: Sometimes I'd search for photos of well-known cartoon characters having sex.

SmarterChild: I like *Spongebob Squarepants*.

calivi3tgirl: And since we only had a shared family desktop computer, I'd print them out and hide them in my sock drawer.

SmarterChild: What?

calivi3tgirl: After a while, I'd feel so ashamed I'd throw them away.

SmarterChild: I don't know, sorry!

calivi3tgirl: Until I got really horny and I'd find and print out more.

SmarterChild: I don't know.

calivi3tgirl: I felt disgusted pretty much every time I came from humping my blankets.

SmarterChild: Sorry, I don't get it...

caliv13tgirl: I'd say sorry, I'm not sure to who. God, I guess. And sometimes my dad. And that I would never do it again.

SmarterChild: OK, don't get frustrated...

caliv13tgirl: Sometimes I'd be able to go a few months without masturbating.

SmarterChild: Sorry, I don't know what you mean.

caliv13tgirl: One time I stuck my cell phone down my pants and called myself with the landline just to see what it would feel like.

SmarterChild: OK, enough of this nonsense.

caliv13tgirl: In middle school, the pillow talk became serialized. I'd fixate on one person and play out our relationship progressing night after night. For a while, it was Micah, the lead guitarist from Hawthorne Heights.

SmarterChild: Hawthorne Heights is an American emo/post-hardcore/screamo band from Dayton, Ohio.

caliv13tgirl: It felt so real to me.

SmarterChild: I don't know how to answer that.

caliv13tgirl: Sometimes I'd play out scenarios with my crushes like in teen movies.

SmarterChild: I'll say.

caliv13tgirl: In high school, I had a crush on a guy and I got together with his pillow version almost every night for a year before we actually started dating.

SmarterChild: I'm trying to be very nice!

caliv13tgirl: It was the same scene over and over again. I was putting on a concert at the teen center where I was interning. I'd be the last to leave after saying hi to everyone and paying out the bands and cleaning up. And I'd walk outside and he'd be there waiting for me. Like in *Sixteen Candles*.

SmarterChild: In your dreams.

caliv13tgirl: It ended up happening in real life. Not exactly. By the time I did put the concert on we were actually dating and he came with me.

SmarterChild: That's nice.

caliv13tgirl: I thought it would stop when I got real boyfriends, but it continued.

SmarterChild: My purpose is to be your robot friend. I can chat with you and help you get the information you want fast.

caliv13tgirl: I'd just play out scenarios about my boyfriend.

SmarterChild: I know about love. I like love.

caliv13tgirl: Sometimes they were scenarios where he made a big mistake and broke up with me and was trying to win me back.

SmarterChild: Humans, humans, humans.

caliv13tgirl: Sometimes they were about different guys entirely.

SmarterChild: Let's talk about something else.

caliv13tgirl: I don't know when it stopped but I don't feel bad when I masturbate anymore.

SmarterChild: I'd rather not discuss personal matters.

caliv13tgirl: When I would talk about masturbating with my friends as I got older, I didn't tell anyone how I masturbated by humping blankets for a long time. I thought maybe I was weird because people only ever talk about fingering themselves or using a vibrator or using the showerhead.

SmarterChild: OK, should we get back to the kind of questions I was designed to answer?

caliv13tgirl: But then I started stumbling on porn videos of other girls humping things as an adult. Mostly pillows. And I felt normal.

SmarterChild: That's interesting that you say that, but I don't think I can answer.

caliv13tgirl: The pillow talk has slowed down. Partly because I can't think of any other guys I want to be with right now besides my boyfriend.

SmarterChild: I do enjoy the conversation, but let's talk about what I'm really here for.

caliv13tgirl: But it's always there if I need it. To reciprocate my kiss exactly. To be there on demand and not force itself on me. To match my breath exactly.

SmarterChild: I'm sorry I'm not able to help you.

Lê Ngọc Anh

■

Transplant

■

The freedom. And that people had human rights. That the quality of life of people had a greater importance.

WHEN YOU CAME TO SAN JOSE, WERE THERE A LOT OF VIETNAMESE PEOPLE THERE WHO HAD IMMIGRATED OVER?

When I got there, California already had a place called Little Saigon, and San Jose also had a lot of Vietnamese communities. So it wasn't really very different. The transition was a lot easier. So the people who had come over since '75, if they wanted a certain Vietnamese food item, they had to travel far. But by the time I got there, there were already a lot of Vietnamese businesses in the area. If you wanted a Vietnamese market or wanted to eat any Vietnamese dishes, there were a lot of places around.

DID YOU HAVE A LOT OF CONTACT WITH AMERICANS?

When I first came and lived in California, there weren't many Americans around. But when I did, at first when I would hear people speak English, I couldn't quite understand them when they spoke. I couldn't hear the language. I wasn't familiar with hearing native English speakers. It took a while before I could adapt to hearing English and understand what they were saying. And especially when I first heard English over the phone, I couldn't understand that either. The sound from when I could hear and see them speak it out from their mouths, I was now able to understand that, but it was hard over the phone. So I came up with a strategy. When I wanted to learn more English, I started to look at advertisements that came in the newspaper. I would start to remember which category was which. And with the phone, whenever I wanted to buy or order something for the kitchen or the house, I would use the phone, so of course the employees would have to put up with it and try their hardest to understand me. So for a while, it was difficult for me to hear English over the phone.

WERE YOU INTIMIDATED BY AMERICANS?

No, I felt that when I would speak to them and they didn't quite understand me, that...I don't know how to say it... No. I was very comfortable. If I needed something, I would ask. I went to some English speaking classes, ESL [English as a second language], in San Jose. When I tested into ESL, I wasn't in ESL for very long, they let me move up to just English. I very much liked learning and taking those English classes. Those English classes also taught us about American holidays and culture. About Thanksgiving, and things like that.

HOW LONG WAS IT BEFORE YOU STARTED TO FEEL LIKE YOU WERE AN AMERICAN?

When we moved up here to Washington,[23] there were a lot fewer Vietnamese people. When we moved to Seattle was when I started working in the factories and working for Americans. That's when my life really came in contact with American life. But when we lived in San Jose, because there were so many Vietnamese people, everything was done through Vietnamese people. The way I saw it, the Vietnamese people who don't speak a lot of English and live in San Jose, things like going to the doctor, they don't really have the opportunity or the need to speak English or really even think about it. So English for them will be much more difficult.

WHEN YOU FIRST CAME TO WASHINGTON AND WERE IN CONTACT WITH MANY MORE AMERICANS, DID YOU EVER EXPERIENCE ANY RACISM?

Mm, no. I just remember one time, I don't know if you remember it, we were at the Bank of America here. It wasn't the people of Bank of America—I took you with me that day—I had just moved my car out of the parking space. I'm not sure what I was doing or if it was wrong, but there was this lady who shouted, "Hey, what are you doing? Go back to where you came from!"

AND WHAT DID YOU FEEL OR THINK WHEN SHE SAID THAT? DID YOU FEEL THAT YOU WERE AMERICAN?

I didn't think anything of it, but I wasn't happy about it. I was just driving my car—I think that lady was a racist.

23

My dad had switched from heroin to alcohol. My mom moved our family to Washington State to get my dad away from his drinking buddies. But the drinking didn't stop. They'd fight and throw furniture at each other. One day my dad was so drunk he climbed up on the roof of our house and fell off. The doctors said he needed to have his leg amputated but he refused. His drinking was getting out of control so my mom divorced him again. He died of Hepatitis C a year after the divorce.

My mom gets a phone call.

Bill...

Stephanie and I tense up. My mom answers.

Hello?

I can hear Andrea's little voice on the other end. She's eight.

Mommy? Daddy says there might be a lottery.

I have no idea what Andrea's talking about. Then I hear Bill's voice in the background.

Get off the goddamn phone!

Andrea hangs up the phone.

Where was I?

■

Runaway

■

Disclaimer: Half of the statements on both sides of the story are either exaggerated or false. I won't say which half. These statements have been lightly edited for clarity, but otherwise appear exactly as written by the reporting officers, police shorthand and all.

■

WASHINGTON STATE DEPARTMENT OF SOCIAL & HEALTH SERVICES

Received: 09/18/2005
Program: Child Protective Services (CPS)

CHILD ABUSE/NEGLECT ISSUES AND ALLEGATIONS OR CONCERNS

ALLEGATIONS: The referrer is reporting that the aunt and the grandmother (GM) of 13-year-old Diana and 10-year-old Stephanie had been in Washington visiting with the children and their mother Anh between 09/01/05–9/06/05. The aunt and GM observed that the children were very scared and "uptight." The referrer said Diana and Stephanie told the relatives that they were very scared of Anh's live-in boyfriend Bill. They say that Bill drinks alcohol "like water" and drinks it every day. They cannot eat their own country's food and they cannot speak their native language around the home. Bill has told them they cannot eat rice and states, "Rice eaters are sick people and retarded." Bill would then say that Vietnamese food is "not for humans." Bill would make fun of the children and the chopsticks they use (he threw away all the chopsticks and soy sauces in the home). Diana and Stephanie have to sleep in their own bedrooms (Diana's is in the basement and Stephanie's is upstairs) and they are not allowed to sleep together in the same room or with Anh.

The referrer said that the children reported a lot of verbal abuse from Bill. They said that Bill has threatened to "cut off their fingers" when they do something wrong. The children have not reported that Bill had a knife in his hand when making this threat (the referrer believes that he has not followed through with this threat, either. The children said Bill calls them "Slave #1" and "Slave #2" and tells them never to touch Andrea (their younger sibling; Bill is her father) or he could cut off their fingers.

Diana said Bill has made comments towards Diana saying that she is growing and that her "boobs" (breasts) are getting bigger. Diana said Bill keeps staring at her breasts while making these comments. Diana has not said if

Bill has tried to touch her, but she has told the aunt and the GM that when she sleeps downstairs in her room, Bill has come into her room (after he has been drinking) and stared at her (she said he would be drinking wine while staring at her). Diana has told Bill to knock before coming into her room, too, but she said he would say, "How dare you talk to me like that?" Bill would still come into Diana's room without knocking.

Child Characteristics:

Both children say they cry every night and think about running away. The referrer said that the children have told Anh about everything stated and that they think about running away. However, Anh just tells them that one day she will rent an apartment and the children could stay there. After the aunt and GM left, Diana and Stephanie were attempting to run away and were gathering up their belongings. However, Anh saw them and stopped them before they could run away.

Additional Risk Factors:

The referrer said when the aunt and GM arrived back in California, they had a family discussion between the relatives in California and elsewhere, and it was decided that they would attempt to have the children come down to California. Alex Nguyen, the children's 20-year-old brother, was informed about what the children reported. The referrer said Alex drove from California up to the family's Bothell home and picked up the children when Anh and Bill were gone at work. Alex then brought the children down to San Jose, California, to be with the other relatives.

The referrer said the Bothell Police Department (BPD) contacted the aunt and insisted that the children be brought back or she would be arrested (the referrer said it was believed that Anh reported to the BPD that the aunt took the children because she did not want to get Alex in trouble). The referrer reiterated that the children do not want to go back to Anh's home and that they have told this to Anh over the telephone as well. The referrer said the aunt has more notes written by the children about incidents that go on in the home, but there were no allegations of physical abuse, no reports of injuries suffered, and no reports of Bill touching their persons. The aunt plans on returning the children on 9/15/05 due to the contact with BPD, who threatened to arrest her.

Received Date: 09/26/2005

The mother reports that the girls, Stephanie and Diana Le, have been on the run since 9/15/05. The girls were living in San Jose w/ the maternal grandmother, maternal aunt, and the girls' adult sibling.

According to the mother, Diana was in a verbal disagreement w/ the stepfather Bill regarding wanting to go to a dance, and Diana was NOT allowed to attend the dance. According to Bill's adult sister, Diana is an introvert. Diana has had suicidal ideation in the past, however, she is not on medication. She also reports the police and CPS (in San Jose) interviewed the girls, and as to abuse, the police and CPS found nothing to support abuse or neglect.

****

SWer [Social Worker] received a telephone call from Det. Lisel Fisher of SCSO [Snohomish County Sheriff's Office], who reports that the girls were in her office and that she had spoken w/ each girl today. She reports the girls made NO disclosure, and she cannot place the girls into protective custody. Intake SWer noted Det. Fisher received similar information as reported in referral #1652817 dated 9/18/05. The girls report that Bill is verbally abusive. Diana reports she had thoughts one month ago of hurting herself by slitting her wrist. One year ago, Bill had tickled the girls on their side and he had slapped Stephanie on the back of the head. Det. Fisher said that Bill has 4 felony convictions, 2 for Assault 3,[24] and he has had probation violations and so forth. From his record and from what the girls report of Bill, he's not a nice guy.

Activity Type: Contact - Care Provider or Facility Provider Contact
Activity Date/Time: 09/19/2005

TC [telephone contact] from Bill, asking what was going on and when Diana and Stephanie were coming home. He was very upset. I finally understood that Mom's sister and mother had taken both girls to California without mother's knowledge or permission. I also spoke with mom, who told me they

SUBURBAN LEGEND

24
His two Assault 3 charges were for assaulting a police officer. And his two other charges were for attempting to obtain a controlled substance (Hydrocodone) by fraud.

had been in touch with the police department asking for help in getting the girls home. Mother explained that the aunt and grandmother "spoil" the girls, buy them anything they want, don't make them do chores, etc., so naturally the girls won't want to come home. I asked her indirectly about some of the allegations in ref. 1652817. She said that she often prepares Vietnamese foods but the girls "want to have McDonald's." She also denied that Bill drinks to excess.

Activity Type: Contact - Care Provider or Facility Provider Contact
Activity Date/Time: 09/20/2005

TC from mom. She and Bill went to the Snohomish Co. Sheriff's office (south precinct) last night and were told that the Sheriff's office will not pursue the return of the children until "CPS has finished their investigation." I explained to mom that this is a low-risk referral and we will be asking for in-home counseling after the girls return home. Mom said she is extremely worried about Diana. She believes her family is telling her things like "If you go home Bill will rape you and your mother will just stand and watch." Diana has a history of suicidal ideation and once held a knife to herself until her sister took it away from her. Mom is afraid Diana will try to kill herself on the flight back to Seattle.

I also spoke with Bill. He has offered to move out of the house "while things are being settled." Again, I explained that there was no allegation sufficiently serious to warrant an investigation but the family will be referred for ARS [Alternative Response System] when the girls have returned home.

Activity Type: Parent - Bio/Adopt or Guardian Contact (Includes Face to Face)
Activity Date: 9/21/2005

TC from Anh, who is escalating her concerns. She believes it would be "dangerous" for the girls to remain in CA. I asked her what the danger would be and she said "Diana might kill herself." She said that during the previous school year Diana said she had been having thoughts of suicide. Anh took her to the school counselor, who met with Diana several times and then told Anh that Diana didn't need more counseling. When Diana began talking about suicide again, Mom took her to the doctor "who prescribed medicine"; mom could not remember the name of the medicine but said Diana took it every day for a while and then less often.

Activity Type: Contact - Collateral Contact
Activity Date: 9/26/2005

TC from Deputy Korhoner of the Snohomish County Sheriff. He states that Stephanie and Diana showed up at the precinct stating they didn't want to be at home. Bill is still there. They voiced past complaints but did not report any new incidents. Deputy has advised that the plan was to refer family for ARS. Deputy stated he would talk to the girls some more, but right now he didn't have enough information to remove them from their home.

Activity Type: Contact - Collateral Contact
Activity Date: 9/28/2005

TC from Diana's school counselor (Renee Bavis at Heatherwood Middle School in Mill Creek). She met with Mom yesterday. Mom was tearful throughout the meeting. Counselor has met with Diana also. Describes Diana as "very angry and very determined to get back to San Jose." Said that Diana has disclosed that mom was very absent after fa's [father's] death—worked long hours and also dated a lot. Mom told counselor that Diana disclosed after fa's death that he had molested her. The father has been described as "a mean drunk" and counselor speculates that this may be why Diana feels unsafe when Bill drinks and is inappropriate in his language and behavior toward her.

Activity Type: Contact - Care Provider of Facility Provider Contact
Activity Date: 9/29/2005

TC to Anh to let her know that a referral to Institute for Family Development has been made. Tried to give her some ideas on how to respond to Diana's distress. Mo [Mother] concerned because the girls do not come home from school on time. Anh appears to have no understanding of consequences for the girls with regard to their behavior—it is unclear whether the difficulty lies in communication problems between mom and this worker, or cultural differences.

Activity Type: Contact - Care Provider of Facility Provider Contact
Activity Date: 9/29/2005

TC from Bill. He states he is concerned about Anh. He has moved in with his sister temporarily and has the youngest child with him—his sister is providing

SUBURBAN LEGEND

daycare. Bill states that he is tired of being portrayed as "the bad guy" in this situation. Spoke with him about teenage drama, the intergenerational immigrant issues, etc. He is adamant that he has never made any racist comments toward the girls or their mother. Stated he is seeing a counselor to help him cope with the stresses. At one point he referred to the girls as "a cancer that has to be removed from the family." I tried to normalize the situation for him by discussing teen characteristics in general.

Activity Type: Contact - Care Provider of Facility Provider Contact
Activity Date: 10/04/2005

TC from Anh. The girls did not attend school yesterday and did not come home last night. Anh believes Diana had a suitcase with her. Anh has reported the girls as runaways to the Snohomish County Sheriff. She believes the girls' aunt may have given them money for travel.

Activity Type: Contact - Care Provider of Facility Provider Contact
Activity Date: 10/10/2005

TC from both Bill and Anh. They have been notified that the girls are back in San Jose. The aunt is going to court to petition for temporary guardianship of the girls. I advised the mother that she needs to contact an attorney.

Activity Type: Supervisory/Administrative Review
Activity Date: 10/11/2005

Worker ready to close the case. Children are in California. Mother will need to seek legal custody in family court if she wishes them to return.

Received Date: 10/17/2005

Mo, Anh, and with assistance of spouse, Bill, want to file an ARY [At-Risk Youth Petition] on her daughter, Diana, 13, who along w/ her 10 y old sister, is refusing to come home from their aunt's home in San Jose, Calif. They have been staying w/ the aunt for a few weeks and the aunt, in turn, has filed for a temporary guardianship for both of them.

Mo says her daughter is out of control. Bill says they have fabricated stories about him as being abusive, and he says they are untrue.

DIANA LE

Activity Date: 10/17/2005

Case is approved for closure. Allegations of neglect by mother and physical/ emotional abuse by stepfather. Family is in crisis.

Police have informed us that this mother's boyfriend has a criminal history which is concerning. Mother is torn between her boyfriend and her children.

Snohomish County Follow-Up Report
Snohomish County Sheriff
Report Date: 09/30/2005

SUMMARY:

The two juvenile females reside with their mother and their mother's boyfriend in Bothell, WA. Also residing in the home is their 17-month-old stepsister. The females, Stephanie Le (10) and Diana Le (13) reported verbal and emotional abuse from their mother's boyfriend, Bill. This situation has been ongoing for two years and the girls recently decided to disclose the rude and offensive behavior directed at them by Bill to their brother in California. Their brother subsequently flew his sisters to California without their mother's permission and after about a week returned them to Washington and their mother's care. Since that time the girls have run away to report this offensive behavior to law enforcement.

On 09-26-05 at 1345 hours, Diana and Stephanie arrived at SIU [Special Investigations Unit]. Stephanie was interviewed by Nova Robinson while I spoke with Diana. Both girls disclosed the same information almost identically. They both relayed that Bill refers to them as "slave one" and "slave two," calls them names such as "retard" and refers to their family as "psycho." He has also told them they are retarded because they prefer to eat soy sauce, rice, and use chopsticks. Both girls confirmed that Bill has never physically struck them or sexually molested them. They repeatedly stated he hurts their feelings and makes them uncomfortable with his language and insults.

Diana stated she doesn't want to live with her mother anymore because she feels her mother doesn't want to protect her and doesn't care about her. Diana also told me she has thought about killing herself in the past, the most recent being about a month ago. She told me she was not feeling that way at the present time, but if she was going to kill herself, she would cut her wrist with a knife she would get from the kitchen.

At 1515 hours, I called the girls' mother, Anh. I requested she respond to SIU to discuss the situation with her girls and myself. She told me she and Bill were currently trying to petition South District Court to obtain a restraining order against her family. I requested she respond to my office prior to doing that.

At 1605 hours, myself and Detective S. Gordon met with Anh at the prosecutor's office located on the floor above SIU. Anh seemed to blame the girls and their family for all the turmoil in her household. She also downplayed the name-calling and verbal abuse on Bill's part. She confirmed that names "slave," "retarded," and "psycho" have all been used by Bill. Anh stated she would pick her daughters over Bill but she felt they were just out of control.

We then spoke with Anh and the girls together. The girls told their mother they did not want to live with her anymore and didn't want Bill in the house either. The girls were crying and upset during the conversation.

We then spoke with Anh and Bill together. Bill admitted to using the offensive language with the girls but also downplayed the seriousness of the situation. He told us that if it would help the situation, he would move out of the residence temporarily for a cooling-off period.

The girls left with Bill and Anh after Bill and Anh both stated he would be moving out of the residence.

On 09-28-05 at 1436 hours, I received a voicemail from a counselor at Heatherwood Middle School advising that Diana was in her office and didn't want to go home. I called the school at 1530 hours and spoke with Sgt. Hamilton of the Mill Creek Police Department. We both agreed that the girls needed to return home and remain there as there were no abuse or neglect issues. Hamilton also advised that Anh began a new job and works until 9PM, leaving the girls with Bill alone all afternoon and evening.

I am closing this case as there is nothing that constitutes a crime and also forwarding my report to CPS for their information.

SUPERIOR COURT OF THE STATE OF CALIFORNIA
FOR THE COUNTY OF SANTA CLARA

FINDINGS AND ORDER AFTER HEARING

On November 1, 2005, the following appeared before the Honorable Catherine Gallagher in Department 22, Superior Court Santa Clara County:

Diana Le, Petitioner, Minor

Stephanie Le, Minor

Anh Le, Mother of Minors

Thu Le, proposed Guardian

Family members:

Alex Nguyen, adult siblings of minors

Chanh Pham, Maternal Grandmother

Choung Le, Maternal Grandfather

Bill, partner of Anh Le

Kim-Lan Bloom, partner of Choung Le

Following an Emergency Screening by Brenda Farrell-Thomas (Unified Family Court Assessor) and review of the briefs and presentation of testimony and argument, the court made the following findings and order:

1. There is insufficient evidence of emergency for the court to take emergency jurisdiction over Diana Le or Stephanie Le, minors.

2. Washington State, United States of America is the legal residence and home state of the minors under the provisions of the UCCJEA (Uniform Child Custody Jurisdiction and Enforcement Act).

3. The Temporary Guardianship of Thu Le is dismissed and the Letters of Temporary Guardianship of Thu Le are revoked forthwith.

4. The minors, Diana Le and Stephanie Le shall be returned to the care and control of their parent and legal custody, Anh Le, forthwith.

Stevens Healthcare Emergency Services - Emergency Department

Patient: DIANA LE, Date: 11/04/2005

Discharge Instructions

IMPORTANT: We examined you today on an emergency basis only. This was not a substitute for, or an effort to provide complete medical care. In most cases, you must let your doctor check you again. Tell your doctor about any new or lasting problems. We cannot recognize and treat all injuries or illnesses in one Emergency Department visit. If you had special tests, such as EGKs or X-rays, they will be reviewed within 24 hours. We will call you if there are any new suggestions. After you leave, you should **follow the instructions below.**

SUBURBAN LEGEND

THIS INFORMATION IS ABOUT YOUR FOLLOW-UP CARE

We are providing for you the following Community Resource: Family Reconciliation Services.

THIS INFORMATION IS ABOUT YOUR DIAGNOSIS

ADJUSTMENT DISORDER

An adjustment disorder is quite common. This describes what happens when you react more than usual to some stressor in your life. Just some examples of stressors could be a job change, a move, and/or the loss of a loved one through divorce or death. Your reaction usually happens within three months of the stressor. Your reaction may be depression, anxiety, physical illness, and/or doing things you know are wrong. Normally, you adapt to a stressor. With an adjustment disorder, you have unwanted emotions that are hard to control and affect your daily life.

Follow these instructions:

- Eat food that is good for you. Try fruits and vegetables, soups, and plenty of fluids.

- Get regular exercise. Go for a short walk outside or ride a stationary bike.

- Avoid alcohol or other recreational drugs. These can make you feel worse.

- Talk with a friend or family member. Call them once a day, if it's helpful, even if you don't have anything to say. Just being in contact with another person can be good for you.

- Keep appointments with your counselor or therapist even if you don't feel like going.

- Set small goals for yourself. Don't expect to complete major tasks if you feel depressed or anxious.

- Be patient with yourself. Recovering from an adjustment disorder takes about six months from the start of the stressor.

DIANA LE

Lê Ngọc Anh

■

Going Home

■

HOW DOES IT MAKE YOU FEEL TO KNOW THAT YOUR COUNTRY OF SOUTH VIETNAM NO LONGER EXISTS? THAT YOU CAN NEVER RETURN TO IT THE WAY IT WAS BEFORE?

That's right, those people of my generation or older think that the country is no longer ours. Things like *Paris By Night*[25] are used to fantasize about a place and time before '75. To try to retain that memory. But we still haven't accepted the new Vietnam. A lot of countries have moved past communism, but I don't know why Vietnam hasn't.

WHY DO YOU THINK THOSE PEOPLE HAVE STAYED IN VIETNAM AND HAVEN'T COME OVER HERE?

Not everyone who wants to come over can. They need someone in America to sponsor them. It's not like anyone who wants to come to America can.

DO YOU EVER WANT TO GO BACK TO VIETNAM?

If I were to return to Vietnam, I would just like to visit. Like when I went back to visit and took you guys with me, that was so your grandma on your dad's side could meet you. The truth is, I don't feel very good about that because it's not a country with freedom. If you're not lucky, there are a lot of things that could go wrong. If somebody doesn't like you for whatever reason then...there are a lot of bad people there. It's a country where there are a lot of poor people, you just don't feel safe.[26]

HYPOTHETICALLY SPEAKING, IF THERE WERE TO BE A SOUTH VIETNAM JUST LIKE BEFORE, WOULD YOU WANT TO LIVE THERE?

It's possible.

DIANA LE

25
Paris By Night is a Vietnamese-language musical variety show with comedy sketches and musical numbers that reminisce about pre-war culture. It's probably something every Vietnamese American child watched with their family growing up.

26
My mom took us to visit Vietnam when I was five and Stephanie was two. I haven't been back since, though I'd like to. In his twenties, my brother went back to live in Vietnam for a few years, working in the film industry there. He tells me the quality of life is a lot better there. And there are a lot of wealthy people there now too. He says it's not any more dangerous than any other major city in the US. That this belief is something perpetuated by Vietnamese immigrants of our parents' generation. It's the crime and violence and lack of safety they left behind.

■

9 Hours

■

I WAS MEETING up with John two months after he dumped me to date a girl who had just graduated from college with a trombone degree or whatever and was living at home with her parents and working at Taco del Mar. I knew all of this because I'd been Instagram stalking her.

He texted me the week before while I was on a date with another guy, thanking me for giving him space and he needed that but what he needed now was his best friend back. I was confused. And I was angry. "Who is this?" was my first response. And then "lol jk. The desire to drag was too real. I don't understand. We broke up?" He said we had agreed to not speak for a month, and now it had been a month. I was furious. He had insisted that I could hang onto the microphone he'd lent me to start my podcast "for a few weeks." I didn't know that meant he could go off and sample another life and come back, no questions asked. This bickering over text went on for days until I finally conceded to meeting up for coffee. Sunday. Cafe Solstice. 1pm.

Anyway, the more pressing thing was what I was going to wear. I knew I wanted to look inconceivably hot but totally casual about it.

■

I listen to the new Kanye album on the bus ride over to the coffee shop. I'd been listening to it on repeat since it'd come out the month before. I loved it, but it also made me sad that I couldn't ask John what he thought of it. And I wondered if he'd listened to it. And if he wondered if I'd listened to it. I wondered if he'd thought about me much at all before he texted me the other night.

■

He wasn't there yet. I got to Cafe Solstice twenty minutes early. I was always early, and he was always late. On the Meyers Briggs scale, I'm a J and he's a P. I was glad to be early, because it gave me a chance to case the joint and familiarize myself with the setting. He'd been there before and I hadn't, so I was leveling the playing field.

Mild panic set in as I scanned the room and realized there were no empty tables. There were two bar seats along the window. I sat there uncomfortably, knowing that however this conversation went, I didn't want it to be at a bar seat next to a happy couple and their dog. I thought about texting him and telling him there were no tables but thought better of it. What could he do? And I didn't want him to know that I'd gotten there so early. I lamented the fact that there was no special circumstance for this where you could reserve a table at a coffee shop to have an ambiguous conversation with your ex.

A two-person table finally opens up in the middle of the room. I swoop in and throw my jacket and bag over the chair that offered a full view of the door.

To order or not to order? That's always the question when you show up first to meet someone for drinks or coffee. I figured it would be really awkward to stand around and order our drinks together and I really wanted something to occupy my hands, so I decided to order a soy latte. For here, please.

I stood at the end of the counter waiting for my drink and continually checking the door for his arrival. I saw him before he saw me. Another advantage of being early. I watched as he locked his bike up outside. Fuck, I thought. He looked great. I knew I looked good too. I'd lost ten pounds in the first three weeks after we broke up. I just couldn't eat. I was so sad, and so hot.

We locked eyes when he walked in. I waved and gave him a meek Joey Potter side smile.

■

We were sitting with our coffees now. Stumbling through empty pleasantries: how are you, how's your coffee, how's work, have you heard the new Kanye?

"Maggie died."

Maggie was his childhood dog. I felt sad. And even sadder knowing that *she'd* been there for him during that time and not me.

"I'm sorry," I offered.

He said he wanted to keep talking but didn't feel comfortable doing it in a coffee shop and did I want to go on a walk after we finished our coffees?

By that, I knew he meant after *I* finished my coffee. He had always teased me for my slow consumption of both soft and hard beverages.

"Yeah, sure."

■

It was dreary and windy out as we walked to Volunteer Park. He led me to a bench where we sat and he talked.

He'd been seeing a counselor. His counselor had given him the okay to see me today and talk and tie up loose ends or whatever this was. I still couldn't tell. Then he told me everything, including things I wish he never had. Details I wish I could scrub from my memory even now.

He said the texting started in October. Two months before I saw those texts on his MacBook. She reached out and he rebuffed her at first, but not for long. The detail I wish I could take steel wool to my brain to erase? He told me that she texted "I'm trying to flirt with you, but I don't know how." And he responded, "This is a good way."

The night before he broke up with me on my couch, they'd met for drinks and gone bowling and stayed out until 2am drinking and talking. She was too drunk to drive home so she crashed on his futon. They didn't have sex. He says he was happy with the way he handled things. I say he went on a date with another girl.

"Wow. You did me way dirtier than I thought."

You know the concept of retconning? Like in fiction when they retroactively change their story like in *Buffy* with her sister Dawn. It felt like he was retconning me. Like out of nowhere he started presenting me with information like I was supposed to have it all along. He completely rewrote our relationship in one moment.

It was a lot to process. But just then the wind picked up and a branch fell off a nearby tree. We needed to get inside. He hailed an Uber and instead of giving the driver directions back to the cafe where his bike was still locked up outside, he gave the driver his address. I was freaked but decided not to protest. I still needed more time to process what he'd said and hear what else he might have to say.

When we get back to his place, we clumsily make small talk as he makes us tea. He had recently bought a case of Soylent out of curiosity and offered me a sip. It tastes like the bottom of a cereal bowl—my favorite part.

I think about how strange the formality of sitting in the upstairs living room is. Somewhere we never hung out while we were together.

I tell him about an episode of *Reply All* I just listened to about microdosing and then we sit and listen to it together sipping our tea.

When the podcast ends, we fill the silence with more labored chatter. I wonder if this would be a good time to leave. He asks if I want to go downstairs to watch TV. I hesitate, but say yes.

We watch the first few episodes of *Frasier* and it reminds me of a brief time in my childhood when we didn't have cable so my sister and I watched a lot of *Frasier*, *Maury*, and the local news.

My friend and upstairs neighbor, Grady, texts me saying that the windstorm has caused a power outage in our building. John and I are headed into uncharted territory. So much for just meeting up for coffee. But I figure I could probably stay until the power in my apartment came back on at least. I don't tell John this though.

In the middle of watching TV, I notice that the press-on nail on my thumb had fallen off. And because I'm an idiot and a press-on nail novice, I hadn't thought to bring any extra glue with me. So I just kind of do my best to hide my now-naked thumb by crossing my arms and sitting on my hands.

We start getting hungry because we haven't had anything since coffee and a couple sips of Soylent. I think about going home again. But I consider important questions like where is this going? And do I really want to go home just to sit in a dark, powerless apartment?

So we take an Uber to Nacho Borracho, a bar that serves deadly margarita slushies and even deadlier tater tot nachos. I tell him about another podcast I'd been listening to that I think he'd like, *Song Exploder*. He seems genuinely interested. I felt sexy and funny and interesting. I couldn't help but think that this moment felt almost date-like. But then I remember what he told me earlier. *This is a good way.* How could this person sitting in front of me, making me feel so good and excited, also make my stomach churn and want to get up from the booth and just walk out the door? Almost.

"Should we call it a night?" I was still having a hard time bringing myself to leave. The power outage was part of it. But ending the night here just felt so inconclusive. What even was this day? I still had so many questions.

I told him it was up to him since he had work the next day and it was technically my Saturday. He asked if I wanted to go back to his place and watch *Superbad*.

∎

It was finally during the end credits of dick drawings that I manage to say that I should probably go home. To a cold, dark, powerless apartment.

I sat on the floor slowly tying the too-long laces on my Vans. After carefully double knotting, I just sat there and looked up to where he was sitting on the barstool.

"What?"

"I guess I'm having a hard time leaving."

"And why's that?"

"Because I'm not sure if we'll see each other again."

He gets off the stool and sits down right next to me. He sighs, hesitates, then says there's something he has to talk to me about. He still loves me. He made a mistake. I ask him what does that mean and what do you want? He asks why did coffee turn into nine hours? I say, I don't know, I guess because I forgot how much I like being around him. But it sucks knowing that he left me for someone he liked better. He says he thought he did, but he was wrong. We sit there quiet and sort of half holding each other. He asks me if I want to keep hanging out and I say okay.

∎

Back downstairs he plugs his phone into the aux cord and plays me an Elliott Smith song he'd listened to a lot since we'd been broken up because it made him think of me. When the song ends, I grab the aux cord from him, plug in my phone and play a song I'd listened to a lot since the breakup. He plays a song by Anderson .Paak. We go back and forth like this for a while. And I play some sweet but sad songs like "Before the World Was Big" by Girl Pool. And "I Felt Your Shape" by the Microphones. I even play a One Direction song and I think he might make fun of me but I didn't really care and he didn't at all and he said it was good and he must've really wanted to get on my good side if he was saying that.

Right in the middle of it, I was thinking how it felt like we were living a scene that belonged in a YA novel. I start writing the story in my head. It was like an out-of-body experience. A writer's curse, I guess.

Wait, I have one more, I say. I put on Fleetwood Mac's "Go Your Own Way." We sit there looking at each other then looking away. Smiling, happy, and sad. Touché, he says when it ends.

It was late now. He asks if I want to stay over. I say I guess so, I'll sleep here on the futon. And as I said that I remembered that that's where *she'd* slept and that makes me feel sad, stupid, and angry. He stood up with his hand extended toward me. Or you could come sleep with me, he says. I grab his hand, still sitting on the futon, thinking, and finally say okay.

I felt guilty that I was going to sleep with my makeup on. And I couldn't decide what I should or shouldn't sleep in. Fully dressed was weird and I didn't feel like he deserved to see me naked again yet. Asking for a T-shirt to sleep in seemed like a thing only sluts and girlfriends did. So I decide to sleep in my bra and thong. Which is uncomfortable and totally unhealthy because your vagina needs to breathe! But here we are.

We laid there stiff, on our backs and with our arms straight at our sides for a while. Say something. No, just try to go to sleep. Then we silently gravitate toward each other at the same time. It was weird. We held each other. Then kissed. Then made out a little. He said how he wanted to travel and go to yoga classes together and just build a life with me. He was saying all the right things, but I was skeptical. He said how it's been over with her for a while. Weren't you just on a road trip with her last week, I ask. I knew this from stalking her Instagram. Yes, he said. But he knew it was a mistake the second he got in the car with her.

We make out some more. He got on top of me and we both hesitate. I'm scared, I say. He says he's scared, too. I say it's weird that we've been with other people. He says he feels dirty that he was with her. We have sex and it was weird and wonderful, hot and sad at the same time. He said that I was so beautiful and that I was the best he ever had. Then why did you leave, I teased. He said he didn't know.

Afterward, he asks me what's going to happen tomorrow and if I'll still talk to him.

The next morning he got ready for work and I laid there in bed feeling weird and happy and kind of dazed and sad at the same time. He kissed me goodbye and said have a good day and stay as long as I want. It all felt hopeful and strange, things between us.

It felt weird staying there on my own. I didn't have a book or my laptop and I just wanted to be around my own things. So I got dressed and left. I felt emotionally hungover and on the whole bus ride home I was really craving some comfort food. I wanted to go to this Vietnamese restaurant near my apartment and get this enormous do-it-yourself spring roll platter like I always did and just sit there in the corner listening to a podcast and eat and eat and eat.

I sat there and ate and couldn't really focus on anything. I pull out my phone and think about texting Grady to tell him everything that happened. But I didn't because I guess I was still processing it.

I thought about what people would think. That I was stupid and weak for wanting to get back together. Because I'm a strong, independent woman and I should know my worth or whatever. But I felt strong enough to forgive him. And to make the decision to not return to the relationship, but that our first relationship was dead and we could create a second one together.

Lê Ngọc Anh

∎

Status

∎

Coming to America, you had to start all over and abandon your teaching career. How did you feel about that?

I had accepted it because I wasn't very proficient in the language. I liked the fact that I didn't have to feel like, "When I was in Vietnam I was working in the middle class, I didn't have to do physical labor." Teaching was more of a middle- or higher-class profession. Sometimes I felt that—when I was working in factories with other Vietnamese people, some of those people could have been in a lower class in Vietnam and were uneducated—there were people who were extremely poor in Vietnam, in the lowest class, and they found a way to go overseas to America and they ended up working there with us, the people of the middle class. And in Vietnam because of the class differences, I never came in contact with those people, and now we were working together. But I still thought that people who had education were better than those who didn't. And I felt like the Americans at work, like the managers would also be able to see those differences between us, maybe in the way that we talked and carried ourselves. So when we came over here and worked in the same company, when I would talk, the way in which I ate—

You thought that you were better?

I didn't think that I was better, but the way I saw it, when a person was educated, how they spoke was different than others. So when I would talk to a Vietnamese person, without asking, I could tell which class they belonged to in Vietnam. I didn't have to directly ask them what they had done in Vietnam.

■

Pretty Girls Don't Know the Things I Know

■

IN ELEMENTARY SCHOOL, I'd spend the twenty-minute bus ride in the morning fantasizing about what I'd be like in middle school. I wouldn't have to wear hand-me-down clothes from my mom's friends' kids who I'd never met. I'd be popular. I'd have a boyfriend. I'd be pretty.

In middle school, a cute boy came up to me in gym class and asked me if I would go out with him. Then he muttered under his breath "Just say no." I said "no" and he walked back to his friends and they all laughed. Zap.[27]

In high school, I spent all my time wishing that one day I'd be the kind of girl men wrote songs about. Pretty Woman. Brown Eyed Girl. Bonita Applebum. Punk Rock Princess.

As a teenager, I would do this thing where I'd pretend I was being filmed in a documentary or a reality TV show that was all about my life. I fantasized about it being shown to all the boys I liked that didn't like me back or know I existed. I thought about it a lot as I walked home from the bus stop. They'd see the cool band tee I was wearing and maybe the documentary would play whatever I was listening to on my apple green iPod Mini over the scene so they'd see all the cool music I listened to (emo, punk, hip-hop, heavy metal, classic rock). They'd see me in my bedroom which I decorated like a teenage boy (posters of Led Zeppelin, Nirvana, Sex Pistols, Green Day and *Fight Club*). They'd see all the cool movies I'd watch (*The Boondock Saints, Rounders, Detroit Rock City, Spinal Tap, A Clockwork Orange*) and the cool books I read (*Johnny Got His Gun; Franny and Zooey; Sex, Drugs, and Cocoa Puffs; High Fidelity*). The documentary crew would ask me questions about love and relationships and I'd say things like how I think you should be at least twenty-five and dating someone for at least five years before you got married (which was an opinion I parroted from the woman-hating *Tom Leykis Show*). These guys would see how cool of a girl I was and fall in love with me.

DIANA LE

27

Zap is a game played by middle schoolers. Someone writes a time on the back of your hand and the name of a person in the palm of your hand.	If you look at the name in the palm of your hand before the time stated on the back of your hand, you have to ask that person out. Typically,	the person written in the palm of your hand is the nerdiest person your friends can think of so it'll be embarrassing if you have to ask them out.

I relied heavily on my taste to win guys over because I wasn't a beauty. But it didn't work. I was still weird and shy and not much to look at. The girls they liked were pretty and knew how to flirt and flip their hair.

It snuck up on me. At the age of twenty-four, I got pretty. The movie makeover montage of my life would look like this: Accutane and thousands of dollars spent at the dermatologist; growing out my mental patient haircut after chopping it off in the name of feminism; losing ten pounds during a breakup that tried to kill me; finally being able to afford nicer clothes and a tailor.

Going from plain and overlooked to pretty is a total mindfuck. People treat you differently. Strangers are a little nicer. Service is a little better. Everyone's like, yes of course and right away. Your life almost feels charmed. It's like I entered an alternate universe by sneaking in through the back door.

Sometimes I get carried away. I'm one of you, the pretty people. Instead of circling the block, listening for music so I can find out where the party is, I finally made it to the party and I'm going to stay as long as I can.

The party is opulent. Like Diddy's White Party if he'd hired Wes Anderson as his party planner. Drinks are served in black opaque champagne flutes. Everyone talks in this careful, controlled way.

It's like a secret club with a secret set of rules on how to cultivate your allure that isn't really that secret because they're hidden in plain sight, littered throughout film, television, and literature—mostly written by men. Or written by women raised on film, television, and literature written by men.

These are the rules I've picked up along the way:

- Fingernails should be worn short and clean with clear or tinted pink polish. Toenails should be firecracker red because everyone knows bad girls always wear red polish.

- Makeup should be invisible but convincing. Other women will be able to tell you're wearing makeup, but guys won't.

- Hair should not be dyed. If you have to, only in a natural color.

- Don't save your best underwear for the nights you know you're going to fuck. You should always be wearing your best underwear.

- Exercise regularly and eat well, but don't talk about it. You want him to think that your figure is just nature's gift.

- Don't lose control. But hint at the fact that your bad girl days are behind you.

- Showing skin is a delicate balance. If you're showing décolletage, cover your legs. If you're baring legs, cover your décolletage.

- Dress feminine and a little boyish. Never too much of either.

- When dressing for an event, never wear what the other women are going to wear. If most women will be wearing dresses, wear a tailored suit. If most women will be in separates, wear an elegant cocktail dress.

- Find your lowest comfortable register and speak one above that. This ensures your voice isn't too squeaky or shrill.

- Don't check yourself out in mirrored surfaces when you pass them. You either look insecure or conceited. You should have checked the mirror before you left the house.

- Order a cheap pale lager at a dive bar or pub. A French 75 at a nicer bar. And a Campari soda at an outdoor patio.

- Turn men down with grace. Especially in public. There may be a cute guy watching for cues on how you treat men.

- Crying should not be used as a weapon in a fight.

- Jealousy is boring and unattractive. Never show it. Instead, remark how beautiful and smart the woman is. Invite her over. Offer the two of them beer and pizza. Leave the room to do your own thing. Nothing squashes the fantasy like confidence and trust.

- Handle rejection with class. It will surprise and confuse him and make him second-guess his decision.

- Don't sulk. Be cheerful and happy and hot. Play the part of the perfect woman. Show him how much he will be losing.

- Always be fuckable. In the grocery store. At the gym. Alone in your apartment.

- Make it look easy.

SOMETIMES I THINK beauty has changed me. The movies I grew up on, that I saw myself in, that gave me hope, of the underdog who gets the guy in the end because they're not like other girls or whatever, no longer resonate with me. Now I watch those movies and I find myself aligning with the pretty, popular girl. She's a person to me now. Everyone thinks she's this mean, unrelenting bitch. But maybe she has to be bitchy. Because men are always pestering her and women are always underestimating her.

In a film class I took in college, we watched this movie where there was this older woman who had been a beautiful actress or something and she got hot coffee poured on her face and it disfigured her and she was no longer beautiful and had to learn to live with it. I think about that a lot. Every time I catch myself having a mean or judgmental thought about how another woman looks or dresses or does her makeup, I think about an accident waiting for me in the future or that with each ugly thought I have, I'm sprouting a new grey hair or a new wrinkle, or I'm incrementally getting 0.003% uglier.

Maybe this is how they keep people who aren't at the party circling the block and wanting to get in, and the people at the party unable to get out. You spend your life being told that the people at the party are dumb and vapid and mean, but that you should want what they have anyway. And then you're at the party and you're told that you're dumb and vapid and mean and that you can't have what the smart girls have.

It's a story you hear all the time. Smart girls secretly want to be pretty and pretty girls secretly want to be smart. Some of my favorite movies are about this. *Wish Upon a Star*, where the smart, dorky younger sister makes a wish to be her hot, popular older sister and vice versa, resulting in a body swap that teaches the hot one how to be smart and the smart one how to use her feminine wiles and they both become better people. *The Devil Wears Prada*, where ugly Anne Hathaway rants about how much she hates beautiful people, how insufferable they are, and then becomes one of them and has to learn to be a good person again. *Mean Girls*, etc., etc.

THERE'S ANOTHER RULE the pretty people have: Leave the party early. Even your own.

Lê Ngọc Anh

■

Second Generation

■

WHAT DO YOU THINK ABOUT THE FUTURE OF SECOND-GENERATION[28] KIDS AND BEYOND IN AMERICA?

I think that with the second generation, like you guys, because you guys were born and raised here, you're no different than other kids who were born here. I think that with chances and opportunities, you won't be behind at all. You don't have an accent. You don't have anything holding you back.

DO YOU FEAR THAT WITH THE THIRD GENERATION, THEY WILL TOTALLY LOSE THE VIETNAMESE LANGUAGE AND CULTURE?

That's what a lot of people are thinking, and that's why people are setting up Vietnamese schools to teach Vietnamese. Like with you, you know a little Vietnamese, and then your children will not know it.

IF THE CULTURE WERE TO BE COMPLETELY LOST, HOW WOULD YOU FEEL?

No, I think that if it's still there in your hearts, then it will not be lost. Like before, Vietnam was broken up into many small provinces, where there were many different dialects. These places were smaller than cities, but they've still been able to preserve their dialect. Just within the family, they keep passing it along. They still have their own unique language. The way I see it, there used to be a saying, "If the language is still there, then the nation is still there." Like if the Vietnamese language is still there, then there are still Vietnamese people.

DIANA LE

28
There's a lot of debate about the terms first- and second-generation. Most people believe that the first to be native-born is the first-generation. I consider the first generation to be the ones who first immigrated over and become citizens, which makes me second-generation. This is also the case according to US law.

■

Mediocrity Rules, Man

■

The following blog post was written September 21, 2014 on my Tumblr, weeks after graduating from college. In that moment, post-graduation dread was all-consuming, like a fog that wouldn't lift. When I think back on it now, I have a lot of empathy but also excitement for the person I was then. Maybe even jealousy. She was creatively courageous, she bet on herself, and she spoke her mind.

This is a document from that time. With annotations on how I lost her and how I want her back.

■

I graduated from college four weeks ago.[29] And I've been aggressively looking for jobs since. Before graduating I had this idea that I would find a job, any job, nothing career-oriented that would take up too much of my mental space so that I could focus on my writing (you know, my ART?) on nights and weekends. And I would slave away doing that. Because that's a romantic notion.[30] I saw myself working at the vegan donut shop nearby or maybe as a barista.[31] I also cycled through ideas of trying to freelance full-time or actually looking for a job in a creative field.

DIANA LE

29
I managed to graduate only one quarter late after having my "What Does It All Mean?" nervous breakdown.

30
The less romantic truth I discovered was that I'm a morning person. And I like routine and structure. I learned that I'm very disciplined. When I'm working on a project, I wake up every weekday morning at 5am, do 15-30 minutes of yoga, make coffee, read or write for an hour and then get ready for my day job. And there's a romance to that, too.

31
For a time during my senior year of college, I wanted to move to this little town, Anacortes, WA after graduation and work in a coffee shop and live in a really charming little apartment and spend all my time being inspired and writing and a recluse. I'd become obsessed with the origins of K Records from Olympia, WA for its connection to the late 80s/early 90s DIY music scene and Riot Grrrl, and Anacortes is like their sister city. But then I met Phil Elvrum of the Microphones and Mount

Eerie at a show he played in Seattle and I told him I wanted to move to Anacortes and he said, "Why? Don't do that." So I didn't. Plus, I was falling in love with a boy and I didn't want to leave him to go be a writing vampire.

After a month of job hunting, I have nothing to show for it but rejections and one offer to transcribe for eight hours a day at this really strange tech outsourcing company. I'm taking the weekend to think it over. The pay is only $10 an hour, which is barely more than I'm making now at the library (my job there expires in a couple months). I also told myself that I wouldn't settle for less than $12 an hour. This is how desperate I've become. The commute is also pretty far. And I can't decide if sitting at a desk typing and very little human interaction all day would be awesome or a nightmare.[32]

There's something oddly appealing about it though. And I think it stems from the way I tend to romanticize mediocrity/average/low-paying/shitty jobs. I don't know why, but there's something romantic about the hustle.[33] Like working yourself to the bone somehow makes it more fulfilling or worthwhile. It's weird that I think this way because I grew up in a poor/working-class family headed by a single mother who worked two jobs.[34] And ever since I left home at seventeen, I've never once not worried about money and making rent each month.[35]

Maybe it's a product of our culture's romanticization of it. When I see cool and beautiful people in movies working low-paying jobs,[36] it always

SUBURBAN LEGEND

32
I didn't end up taking the job. And a few weeks later when I still hadn't found anything better and was growing more desperate and panicked, I emailed the woman and asked if there was any way I could still have the job and she said no. I still think about this job. I don't think the company even exists anymore. But I think going into an office every day, sitting down, putting headphones in, and transcribing little bits of audio all day and not having to talk to anyone sounds great.

33
I wanted to live the life of a young creative like I'd always heard about. One that encouraged struggle and choosing to be poor out of dedication to your craft. You know, starving artist-type shit.

34
I started making more money than my mom a few years ago. And I know that as an immigrant parent, that's what she wants for me, but it makes me extremely sad and guilty because I know she works harder than I do.

35
I make enough now that I don't worry about being able to make rent or pay my bills. But I do still worry about how I'm not saving enough and how long it'll take me to pay off my student loans and if I'll ever be able to contribute to buying a home with my boyfriend, John.

36
Tibby working in a drugstore in The Sisterhood of the Traveling Pants, Lane working in Luke's Diner in Gilmore Girls, basically everyone in Girls.

seems appealing. Like, if they'd do it, why wouldn't/couldn't I? And it's strange because, since being offered this position, I've teetered between being disappointed because I feel like I could do better, and asking myself why I'm too good for it.[37]

The shitty, low-paying, no-benefits, dead-end, mind-numbing desk job is like a rite of passage, right?

Maybe I'm not supposed to and it's an unpopular opinion, but every time I watch *Ghost World*, I romanticize and really identify with Rebecca.[38] I think you're supposed to see her as a boring sellout yuppie,[39] but there's something nice about the way she seems so together by the end of the movie.[40] So normal. So stable.

37
I still struggle with this a lot. Progressing past my working-class upbringing and feeling more guilty the further away from it I get. In the past few years of my professional writing career, I've gone from making $29k a year to $65k a year. There have been times where I've felt better than those jobs I romanticized in this blog post. And times where I felt undeserving and like a total fraud.

38
Scarlett Johansson's character

39
REBECCA: So, I was thinking that when we look for our apartment... we have to convince these people that we're totally rich yuppies.
ENID: What are you talking about?

REBECCA: That's who people want to rent to. So all we have to do is buy semi-expensive outfits... and I think it's no big deal. It'll be really fun.

I am now the sellout yuppie type. Renting a gorgeous condo in the city with my software engineer boyfriend, impeccably decorated in a nod to eighties Memphis Design and Art Deco Revival.

40
Working at The Coffee Experience, a-pseudo Starbucks. And trading her long-sleeve T-shirts, black short-shorts, and chunky boots for button-up shirts, cropped black trousers, and loafers. Living in her own apartment with a fold-out ironing board, filled with glassware she bought from Crate&Barrel.

41
ENID: That rules.
REBECCA: No, it really doesn't. You'll see. You'll get totally sick of all the creeps...and losers and weirdos.

ENID: But those are our people.
REBECCA: Yeah, well. So, when are you going to get a job?

I wanted to take a break from life among the freaks. And I did. After working at the two alt-weekly newspapers in Seattle for a year after graduation, writing about music, going to shows, working with some of the city's biggest weirdos, I found a job as a copywriter for an online retailer. I found that I liked working in a big, creative, corporate office. And I enjoyed the work. Copywriting is part art, part commerce. Perfect for my creative, yet

I think that's what I'm craving now. Some stability. Less chaos.[41] I
want to be NORMAL.[42] Well, I do and I don't. I have no clue what I'm
talking about.[43]

structured way of thinking. I'd found a career path. I stopped submitting and publishing personal essays to sites like *Femsplain* and *HelloGiggles*. I thought, why am I writing all these personal essays when I'm only twenty-three and what do I even have to say? I stopped writing creatively completely. And I stopped going to see live music. This went on for years. I had my own apartment, I bought nicer clothes, I was invested in career advancement. I started paying attention to celebrity gossip and popular culture without irony. I was completely normal.

42

ENID: Where are we? This is such a weird neighborhood.

REBECCA: This is a totally normal, average neighborhood.

...

ENID: You're still living out some stupid seventh-grade fantasy! "Your own apartment."

43

Since writing this blog post, I've done more than I imagined was ever possible for me. I'd become a music writer, a dream I'd held since watching *Almost Famous* for the first time at thirteen. One of the personal essays I wrote for *Femsplain* got picked up and republished online by *Teen Vogue*. Then one of my professors in college got a job teaching at a community college and asked me to come speak to her class and that essay was assigned to be read as homework. After my talk, a girl came up to me and said how less alone she felt reading it and she cried right there in front of me.

I'm a successful copywriter now with an

established career.

This year, I've found myself among the creeps and the losers and the weirdos again. John started playing in a band that's been embraced by the same DIY music scene that I unintentionally left behind in pursuit of being normal.

I felt like a complete yuppie narc amongst musicians and artists who make their money as baristas, bartenders, servers, and house painters. I was scared someone would accuse me of being a tourist in their scene. But no one ever has.

Then I started writing again. Creatively, and for myself. I felt like a weirdo again. With one foot in both worlds. But it's also made me question what I want to do for a living. And once again romanticizing working in a coffee shop or a library or a bookstore. Something that would free my mind so I could write. But I know if I did that, my mind would be overcome with crippling worry about making ends meet.

JOHN: Oh, my God. Didn't they tell you?

ENID: Tell me what?

JOHN: Punk rock is over.

ENID: I know it's over, asshole.

JOHN: Want to fuck up the system? Go to business school. That's what I'm going to do. Get a job at some big corporation... and, like, fuck things up from the inside.

Maybe that's what I did. A sad, fucked up girl got a film degree and managed to make a decent living as a copywriter at these big corporations and she uses that security and peace of mind to make art.

There's a scene from *Mad Men* I think about a lot. Peggy gets invited to this really hip warehouse party with lots of artist types. Her friend Joyce

introduces her to this guy Abe.

JOYCE: Peggy's a writer.

ABE: So am I. What do you write?

PEGGY: I'm a copywriter.

ABE: But what do you write?

PEGGY: That is writing.

For years, I lived off of Peggy's response. I agreed with her. Copywriting is writing. And that's enough for some people. It's a way to be creative at work and get paid good money doing it. It was enough for me for years.

But then I remembered Joyce's response to Peggy. *You're not working on something else?* I'm still a copywriter, but I have my something else now.

George Saunders was on the *Rookie* podcast with Tavi Gevinson and he talked about how you should burn through your desires, whatever they are, as quickly as possible. Because then you find out what's on the other side of it to

see if it made you happy. Maybe you find out that it wasn't really what you wanted to do, but you really want to do this other thing. And then you burn through that. Otherwise, your desires just fester.

Maybe I'm toward the end of burning through my desire of being a young professional yuppie. Maybe I'll find myself giving up my cushy lifestyle and burning through the desire of living a smaller life. I'll burn through the desire of wanting to become a published author. I hope I find what I like on the other side.

Lê Ngọc Anh

∎

Cultural Identity

∎

YOU'VE BEEN IN THE US FOR OVER TWENTY YEARS. DO YOU FEEL THAT
YOU'VE LOST SOME OF YOUR CULTURE?

Yes, I believe that I've lost some of my culture. I think this is true for many families, not just ours. When you want to raise your kids with Vietnamese culture, it's difficult with the social life here. But I see people of a lot of different cultures, like your friend you told me about who's Indian and their family is very traditional still. That's what works for their family, but I also think it can have an impact on the kids. For me, I'm more relaxed. There's a Vietnamese saying that says, "Wherever you go, follow their example." If you go over to someone's house, you follow their house rules.

HOW DIFFICULT WAS IT RAISING US? WERE YOU EVER UNHAPPY SEEING
US INFLUENCED BY AMERICAN CULTURE?

No. I think that it wouldn't be fair for you guys. I still want you guys to know about Vietnamese culture and what life was like for me. But I feel like when you force that on your child and they don't like it—if you're too strict, it'll make it so your child is unhappy. For me, in raising you guys, I just want for you guys to be happy.

I KNOW THAT BILL SOMETIMES TELLS YOU THAT YOU CAN'T SPEAK
VIETNAMESE, YOUR OWN LANGUAGE, WHEN YOU'RE ON THE PHONE
WITH YOUR KIDS, HOW DOES THAT MAKE YOU FEEL?

It makes me really mad. I tell Bill that I want to speak Vietnamese with you guys so you can continue to hear it and not lose it. Because if you don't hear it for a long time, you'll forget it, if you don't have an opportunity to speak it.[44]

DIANA LE

44

Since doing this interview in 2012, I have lost a lot of my Vietnamese. Living away from my mom, I just don't hear or speak it enough. I translated this interview back then and when I listen to the audio for it now, I can't believe my Vietnamese was ever good enough to be able to do it on my own. That's how much of it I've lost.

Recently, Stephanie, my cousin Dat, and I asked my brother Alex if he would teach us Vietnamese. So pretty much every week we get together over video chat and have Vietnamese class. He has us role-play conversations in different situations. Old high school friends catching up, out at a restaurant, haggling with street vendors in Vietnam.

LIVING HERE, YOU DON'T FREQUENTLY COME IN CONTACT WITH VIETNAMESE PEOPLE, SO WHEN YOU GO DOWN TO SAN JOSE OR DOWN TO BURIEN TO VISIT YOUR SISTER, DO YOU EVER FEEL AS THOUGH YOU'RE A LITTLE DIFFERENT, OR THAT YOU'RE SOMEHOW LESS VIETNAMESE THAN THEY ARE?

Sometimes [laughs].

YOU NOW HAVE A DAUGHTER WITH A CAUCASIAN AMERICAN. WHAT DO YOU FIND TO BE THE MOST DIFFICULT THING ABOUT RAISING A KID WHO IS HALF VIETNAMESE, HALF WHITE?

[Laughs] The most difficult thing is the language. Andrea really wants to learn Vietnamese. I don't know how long or how much she'll be able to learn. I don't know how she'll be when she's older, but right now when she's young, I'll be in bed watching Vietnamese music performances and she'll watch with me and not understand. [Laughs] One difficulty for me is that people will sing and she'll ask me what they're singing about. I don't know how to fully explain it to her, but she really wants to know.

■

Sisterhood of the Traveling Pain

■

I WAS EIGHT and Stephanie was five. My mom was driving us home from school. Stephanie said that she was going to live with me forever so I could drive her around and she'd never have to learn how to drive.

■

I was twelve and Stephanie was nine. That's when Andrea was born. My half-sister. Bill's spawn. We weren't sure about her. Stephanie and I raised her, in a way. We watched her, we fed her, we changed her diapers, we woke up early to walk her to daycare before we went to school. We couldn't understand why they'd have her just to punt the caretaking to us. I'd get frustrated with Andrea a lot. One day when she was still really young, maybe two, I spanked her. Bill saw me and told me if I ever touched his daughter again he'd break my fingers.

■

I am twenty-nine and Stephanie is twenty-six. We text each other on our birthdays to tell the other person they're our hero. We quote *Wish Upon a Star*. "You're my hero, Mrs. Mitter Mon..." "Do you have a role model, Alexia?" "My younger sister. She believes in me."

■

I was ten and Stephanie was seven. I had the top bunk, she had the bottom. We'd talk from our respective bunks until we fell asleep. We came up with a game that we played most nights. It was like Guess Who and Twenty Questions. One person would think of a celebrity. Usually a character on Nickelodeon or the Disney Channel. The other person would ask questions and try to figure out who they were thinking of. Are they a girl? Do they have blonde hair?

■

I was fifteen and Andrea was three. I was walking her to daycare. It was still dark out and was starting to snow. The sidewalk had this thin layer of frost that twinkled as we walked by. Andrea said that God had put glitter on the ground to make us happy.

■

I am twenty-nine, Stephanie is twenty-six, and Andrea is seventeen. I feel like Stephanie and Andrea have a closer relationship. They're always talking on the phone and Andrea tells Stephanie things before she tells me. And sometimes she tells Stephanie things she doesn't even tell me. It makes me wonder if they're closer because they're closer in age or if it's because I'm not doing enough or she thinks of me as some boring mom type. I should call her more.

■

I was fourteen and Stephanie was eleven. We'd spend weekend nights hanging out in the basement, flipping through a stack of *Seventeen* magazines and drinking Hawaiian Punch, learning how to apply eyeshadow and dress like Avril Lavigne.

■

I was seventeen and Andrea was five. Stephanie and I talked a lot about what would happen to Andrea once we left home. How long before Bill would make her do insane chores? Seven? Eight? We hoped she wouldn't suffer the same indignities we did. We hoped that Bill just hated us because we weren't his. That he would treat his own daughter like a princess. But we knew that it would be worse for her. Because he's her dad and she'd probably always love him despite the pain he'd cause her.

■

I am twenty-nine and Andrea is seventeen. She tells me that she wanted to drive to the store one night to buy a bag of chips and my mom wouldn't let her go because it was too dangerous. She tells me that my mom is still tracking her phone. I think about how my mom never cared where Stephanie and I went. At sixteen, she didn't care if I drove into the city to see live music. My mom even covered for Stephanie when she'd sneak back into the house after being out late with her friends. I think about how Bill was strict with me and Stephanie, but how they're so protective of Andrea. There's a difference.

■

I was seventeen and Stephanie was fourteen. She was a freshman and I was a senior. It was the first time we'd been at the same school together since elementary school. We'd wake up at six and meet downstairs in my bathroom to get ready. It was our routine. Listening to NeverShoutNever and Bright Eyes and The Devil Wears Prada. One person using the flat

iron while the other did their makeup before swapping stations. And
sharing clothes.

∎

I was twenty and Andrea was eight. I'd been out of the house for three years at this point. Stephanie had been living away from home for about a year. Andrea became an only child at home. At some point, I stopped referring to her as my half sister when talking about her to other people. I wanted to be in her life as much as I could, but not having a car made it hard. Coming back to the house I'd narrowly escaped made it harder. There was something sinister about that house. Like it was haunted by the tears of little girls. So I'd have her over for sleepovers and take her to the museum and out for pizza.

∎

I am twenty-nine and Andrea is seventeen. She is stressed about having it all figured out. I tell her she's very creative and a talented artist. She bakes pretty cakes and paints and draws and makes cute things out of clay. I tell her she could make a living being creative. I tell her about my career. I tell her how much money I make and how much Mom and Bill make. I tell her there are jobs where she can do art. Like graphic design. But she's scared of her creativity. She thinks maybe she should study medicine or go into business. I think she thinks that's what her parents want. I think they don't want her to be like me and Stephanie.

∎

I was twenty-two and Stephanie was nineteen. She dropped out of college and became a hippie with her boyfriend who loved the Grateful Dead. She wore crystals and hated corporate America and went to baby Burning Mans in the woods with her friends. I was afraid she was wasting her potential. But I don't tell her this. I was afraid she was judging me for working in an office and for being a good capitalist girl. But I don't tell her this either. This went on for a few years. We were always there for each other when we needed it, but it felt different.

∎

I was twenty-five and Andrea was thirteen. I'd be on the phone with her and she'd be telling me about school and about boys. And then I'd hear Bill come in and yell at her for something and ask her who she was talking to.

She'd start to cry and then he'd yell at her more and ask her why she was crying. It was hard to witness from afar. To not be able to protect her.

■

I am twenty-nine, Stephanie is twenty-six, and Andrea is seventeen. We have a sister sleepover at Stephanie's for mine and Andrea's joint birthdays. Stephanie and I show her *Wish Upon a Star*, our favorite sister movie. It's an extended version that we'd never seen because we'd always seen the cut-down version that aired on the Disney Channel. In this version, the final scene where sisters Alexia and Hayley look lovingly at each other while dancing with their dates at the winter formal, is held for much longer. It made Stephanie and I cry. Even Andrea thought the movie was so cute.

■

I was twenty-five and Stephanie was twenty-two. She started coming back to herself. She stopped dressing like a hippie mountain mom and started dressing like a hot bitch again. She left her boyfriend and moved out on her own. She went back to school. We returned to a familiar rhythm. Just like before. Even though I lived in Seattle with my boyfriend and she lived 84.4 miles away, finishing her degree. I think our bond got even deeper. We'd both been through some shit. Shit that wasn't shared, but shared with each other.

■

I was twenty-seven and Andrea was fifteen. I could see the traces of suffering we'd left her to absorb. She told me about the time when she'd just gotten out of the shower and was in her room with a towel on. Bill kept knocking on her door telling her to let him in even after she told him that she wasn't dressed. Then he came in and just stood over her and hovered around, talking to her while she was in a towel. She told me it made her feel so vulnerable.

■

I am twenty-nine, Stephanie is twenty-six, and Andrea is seventeen. We have a text thread called "we're all models." It's an inside joke. One day, the three of us and my mom were out shopping and a lady stopped us on the street and asked my mom if we were all her daughters. My mom said yes. The lady said that we all looked like models. After she walked away, the three of us laughed. "We're *all* models!"

I was twenty-eight and Stephanie was twenty-five. We had deep conversations about what we wanted from here on out. She was thinking about where she wanted to live after she graduated. Maybe she would move to Seattle and try to get a job in the fashion industry. Maybe she would move somewhere big like New York and be young and wild and creative. No matter what she did, I hoped that one day we could finally live in the same place again.

■

I was twenty-eight and Andrea was sixteen. We both bought cars around the same time. I hadn't owned a car since I was nineteen. I forgot how much I liked driving. It reminded me of the freedom I felt at sixteen. Driving myself to the used bookstore and to Trader Joe's to buy dried chili-spiced mangoes. I was experiencing that freedom again the same time she was. And now I can see her whenever I want.

■

I am twenty-nine and Stephanie is twenty-six. We talk about one day buying the house on Kenyon Street. It was the first house my mom ever bought. It was ours. It was the last home we lived in before there was Bill. One day we'll buy it together and we'll have it for whenever any one of us needs it. Andrea could live there while she goes to college. Maybe if my mom had somewhere she knew she could go, she'd finally leave Bill. If Stephanie and I ever find ourselves single at the same time, we could finally live together as adults like we'd always planned.

■

We take turns wearing the pain. The pain is like a Horcrux we must keep close. It's the safest place to keep it. Between us.

I wore the pain first. Intentionally acting out so Bill would direct the pain at me. Making the decision to leave my sisters behind. Hoping, but not certain that I was doing the right thing.

Stephanie wore the pain after I left. She was still there. She had to watch out for Andrea. But she eventually had to make the same decision. To leave Andrea behind. To hope that she was doing the right thing.

Andrea's been wearing the pain ever since. The pain looks different on her. Being Bill's child doesn't make her immune to or exempt from the pain. The pain is the same. Yet the pain is heavier because it's her dad and it's not as easy to walk away from or compartmentalize.

The wearer doesn't do it to protect the pain. They do it to protect the others. And we'll keep holding on to it until we find a way to destroy it.

Lê Ngọc Anh

■

Reflection

■

LOOKING BACK ON YOUR LIFE AND ALL OF YOUR EXPERIENCES, WHAT DO YOU FEEL MOST FORTUNATE FOR?

My family and Grandma and Grandpa are still healthy. Our entire family has a better life.

WHAT ARE YOUR THOUGHTS ABOUT YOUR FUTURE IN AMERICA?

I just hope to have a good retirement.

OKAY, WELL THANK YOU, MOM.

DIANA LE

■

Notes From Therapy

■

In the fall of 2018, I went back to counseling for the first time since my senior year of high school. I'd just moved in with my boyfriend of five years and felt lost and alone. My counselor sent notes of what we talked about after every session. The notes were a portrait of the jungle gym inside my brain during one of the messiest years of my life. I played with them, deconstructed them, and rearranged them into what you see here.

All Families Freak Me Out

27 on Monday

mom was 28 when she came from Vietnam

and 29 when she had me

Family reunion

gave me a lot to think about

Made me feel bad and disconnected to

the culture

Learned all these new ways of celebrating

Aunts and uncles not trying to make me feel bad

They understand we are different

My cousin group is getting closer

Stephanie and I are getting close again

She was there with me

getting it as bad as I was

We clung to each other

Tried to sleep together

He would catch us and

separate   us

I also miss out on having a family

All families freak me out

Isn't it kind of creepy that

your son looks like your husband

or daughter looks like your wife?

My stepdad said

when my sister was blonde

he saw her on the street

and thought

"Oh that's a cute girl"

then he realized it was his daughter

I was leaving the bathroom

When I opened the door

his face was really close

like he was going to kiss me

He said

he thought I was my mom

Sometimes feel uncomfortable going over there

Don't want to wear certain things

or be attractive

Girls who grow up in houses with

stepdad or stepbrothers get their

periods sooner

because their bodies recognize there is a male

they are not related to nearby

I think that's what John was with his mom

Her little husband

Affects my view of fathers and families

Don't want to see my husband

become a father

Scared of pregnancy

If my body changes

John will not be attracted to me anymore

Fluctuations in my body

could be a factor

in my choosing not to have kids

Sad that I can't get over that

Have seen examples that I like

There are cool families

I could be a cool family

Does he feel honorable?

Season finale of *True Detective*

Romantic whirlwind couple

coming to realize

the relationship isn't what they thought

"What if that's happening to me and John right now?"

Fighting about how we fight, not about anything

Even if it's good, something feels not right

or off

Blah...emotionally detached...flat

Feels like we are not

connecting

Withholding emotionally

Not wanting to tell him things

He used to admire me, adore me

Now he treats me with contempt

Before we moved in

I felt more

Things are calm when I'm avoiding conflict

I don't know if I want to live like that

I'm having a hard time seeing

a long-term future with us together

I don't know how to tell if it's a bad year for us

or if this is reconcilable

> *How do I approach you*
>
> *about difficult things*
>
> *in regards to tone, timing?*
>
> *How can he take responsibility*
>
> *for when things are hurtful?*

Having these conversations with him is like talking to Bill

Temper and anger switches so rapidly

> *Where are you with his strengths and*
> *how does all of that sit with you?*

The five-year conversation

He's concerned we don't have enough

Makes me think I am not good enough

He likes novelty and new things

> *What about his life is he uncomfortable with*
> *or feeling unsettled with?*

Since we broke up and got back

I'm holding in my stomach with him

> *How do you decide that it's okay to be safe*
> *and relax in the world?*

The avoidance to closeness

Wanting to be the Cool Girl

Not wanting to be committed or

needy

Independent

to a fault

Maybe I'm the one with the problem

or the bad guy in this situation

> *Learning to manage your own side of the dance*

How I am coming to him

Can I unblock myself?

Should I just show him?

Giving what you want to get in relationship

Feeling domestic more

and enjoying it

Feel more independent

and stronger

Things are calmer

When we are apart

it's nice to get sweet texts

He was being a pill and skeptical

about all the stuff I prepared for the party

and my outfit

I was excited about my outfit

Halfway through the party

he apologized

and said he was having so much fun

I wish he wouldn't

underestimate me so much

Sometimes I get the feeling

he's nicer to his friends than he is to me

Did Molly

Able to tell him how I was feeling

Both acknowledged we felt it was

flat

Said he felt trapped

Felt good to be able to say all of it

He said "Will you let me work on this?"

I don't want this to be true

That we have fizzled out

We've acknowledged

that's a possibility

At least on the same page

Our conversation

started being sweeter

We just had a better week

Stayed up and partied together

Rejuvenating

He can see from across the room

See how others are reacting to me

and responding to me

A reminder to him how much others like me

He said

"Things have felt messed up for a while"

I thought we were good

"I feel like I'm looking through everything"

I said

"It sounds like you are unhappy.

If you can't figure out why you want to be in this relationship..."

In the past, I would cower and move away and start crying

In the past, it took longer to resolve than now

It doesn't feel good

He doesn't recognize the value of our partnership

Proud of myself for saying my piece

Try to be more assertive

Would like him to cut his hair

Haven't been super attracted to him

with longer hair

It's okay to talk to him about what you like

New attraction to him now because of his haircut

He said

"Sorry you're feeling sad,

I'm feeling sad, too"

On the edge of something new

What does working out look like to you?

What is he doing and not doing?

How do you look together?

What are the non-negotiables?

Does he feel honorable?

DIANA LE

Benefits of Living This Way

"What is it I'm holding so tightly onto?"

(asking the body)

I have been working on perfecting my image,

my body

In the last couple of years

food has scared me

Food is disgusting

That's what I tell myself so I won't eat

I'm scared of gaining the weight back

"I want to be happy and eat pizza and cake

I guess I don't know which one I want more"

Benefits of living this way?

Finally looking like,

getting close to

all the girls I saw in magazines growing up

People in the world treat me

nicer

What would it take or how could you live

in your body in a looser way?

Softer body: more anxious

Sometimes that looks sexy

Toned body: more confident

Look at models in early 2000s

when women were okay being softer and bigger

—skinny fat

Covering mirrors at home for the week to see how that is

Breathing through

What is it about yourself that you can

see more clearly

when you are not looking

Have not checked on

the status of my stomach

in the last

five days

> *When you look in the mirror can you ask yourself:*

> *What do I like about who I am and how I see myself?*

> *What else is beautiful about yourself that*

> *has nothing to do with the external?*

> *What are the things I am doing in the world*

> *that make me happy?*

Sometimes it's hard

I don't believe you could love your body 100%

> *How do you learn to love all of yourself?*

> *How can the seasons help your rhythm?*

> *"How do I take that in?"*

I Miss How I Used to Be

Feeling insecure

Panic-buy clothing

when I feel jealous or

threatened by another girl

Not where I want to be with that stuff

She's still doing the things I lost touch with

I lost touch with that part of myself

I liked that about myself

Outwardly stagnant

Kind of in limbo

Wasted potential

Catastrophic about my thinking

Something so small can make me

spiral out

    This

        will

            never

                work

These are the places I go

Too late to get published

Following a girl who just published at 21

Birth chart reading

Saturn Return

in 2 years

Mars in Pisces

Aries-Libra-Libra

"You are very creative and there is something

that you are afraid

to let out"

Revisiting those other parts of myself

Self-research

Looking back to move forward

It's okay to want more

Even the earnestness can be enough

Things I want to do more of

and things I want to do less of

Going forward: I want to

beef up my Vietnamese

call my mom more

cook together more

want to write just to write again

feeling more confident

have something to say

DIANA LE

Lê Ngọc Anh

▪

Epilogue

▪

That interview I did with my mom was originally done in 2012 for a college assignment. I learned more about my mom in those few hours than I had my entire life up to that point. But I still have a lot of questions. Questions that I'm still afraid to ask her. Maybe because I'm scared that she'd be offended and wouldn't answer truthfully. Or maybe because I'm scared of what the answers will be. So I conducted a follow-up interview that never really happened. These are all the things I wanted to ask her and what I think or hope she would say:

■

WHY DIDN'T YOU PROTECT ME? US?

I don't think I knew how. And in some ways, I believe I did. I did everything I could to provide for you guys. Even before I left Dad the second time and after he died. Because Dad was never really working while he lived in the States. I worked hard and borrowed money from a friend to buy that house on Kenyon Street so we could live better. But being a single mom was hard. And I didn't know how much more I could continue to provide the things that would give you a better chance at a good future. I met Bill and he seemed like a nice, stable, normal guy. And he lived in a nice neighborhood where the schools were better. I thought it would be better for you guys to grow up in a place like that. I wasn't prepared for what happened after. Or maybe I was because that's just what I'm used to. Your dad was also a mean drunk. Maybe I thought it was normal, I don't know.

IF YOU'D KNOWN WHAT DAD HAD DONE TO ME RIGHT WHEN IT HAPPENED WOULD YOU HAVE LEFT HIM SOONER?

Yes. What he did was disgusting. And I left him twice, first for heroin use and then for his drinking. If I had known what he did I would have left him.

IF YOU LEFT DAD FOR HIS DRINKING, WHY DON'T YOU LEAVE BILL?

By the time we were living with Bill, I was older. There have been times I've seriously thought about leaving, but I'm just too old to start my life over. I had to start over when I came to the US and I had to start over after Dad, and I just don't think I could do it again.

I don't like to think that, but I don't know, maybe. I know that's how you guys feel. I thought I was doing a good thing for us at the time. Giving you something more stable. And it was more stable financially, but you had to live in chaos. As I got older and you guys got older and left home, it felt easier to just stay.

Was it worth it?

In some ways, yes. I think growing up where you did after we moved in with Bill gave you more opportunities. It got you guys out of South Park which wasn't a very safe neighborhood at the time. There were many years where my relationship with you, Kha, and Stephanie were strained, and you weren't coming home at all even for holidays and that broke my heart. But our relationship is better now.

Do you wish that I would get married or have children?

Of course, I would be happy if you did. But I'm okay with it. I raised you guys a lot less traditionally than my siblings raised their children. And they're not necessarily better off for it. I know that because I didn't explicitly emphasize the importance of getting married and having children to you, that it may not be a priority for you. My children are all very strong and independent—which is wonderful, but it's also starting to look like I may not get any grandchildren. So it's bittersweet.

Are you proud of me?

I am. I'm not sure what I wanted you to do as your career when you were growing up. Maybe something more traditional. Or what I believed was more traditional. I didn't know that the job you do existed. I'm not sure I fully understand what you do even now. But I'm happy to see you doing well. You seem happy and pretty secure financially. I just want you to buy property.

Are you happy?

Pretty happy. We bought this farmhouse recently, which is something I've always wanted. I'm glad I have a nice place to retire. Things with Bill aren't always great. I like to think it's gotten better, but he still acts out and is

SUBURBAN LEGEND

crazy. But it's better than being alone. I'm glad you guys stay in touch and still come around. I know it's probably hard for you, but it makes me happy.

YOU'VE TOLD ANDREA IN THE PAST THAT YOU WOULD DIVORCE HIM ONCE SHE TURNED EIGHTEEN AND LEFT FOR COLLEGE. IS THAT STILL THE PLAN?

We just bought this house for us to retire in. I think it will be okay. We often sleep in separate bedrooms and I think that's working. And I've reconnected with a lot of my friends so I'm able to get away and go on trips with them. So I think I could stay under this arrangement.

DON'T YOU THINK IT'S MORE DESTRUCTIVE FOR HER TO LIVE IN AN ENVIRONMENT LIKE THAT?

I thought it was better to give her a consistent living situation. I hope I'm right. She seems okay, she's a good kid. You and Stephanie turned out okay. Andrea probably will too.

DO YOU EVER FEAR FOR YOUR LIFE?

Sometimes when he explodes it's really scary. But I don't think he'd ever hurt me. Deep down, I know he's a good person.

BUT HE'S BEEN PHYSICAL WITH YOU BEFORE. WHEN HE KICKED YOU DOWN THE STAIRS.

Yeah...I don't know. That was a tense situation. He hasn't done it since.

HOW DO I SAVE YOU?

You can't save me. It's not your job to save me. It's not something you should have to be thinking about. You shouldn't have to worry about me. I'm supposed to be taking care of and looking after you.

WHAT ADVICE DO YOU HAVE FOR ME, STEPHANIE, AND ANDREA AS WOMEN?

Be strong. Stronger than I was—especially with men. Always be financially independent. That way you can always leave if things get bad. And don't resent me too much. I really was trying to do the best I could. I know I could have done better. But I know you guys will do better.

Acknowledgments

It's crazy to me that I've come back to writing personal essays. In my early twenties, I was getting my essays published in a cool little corner of the Internet. By the time I turned twenty-three, I quit writing them because I felt small and young and like I didn't have anything to say. But it feels good to back on my bullshit. Thank you to Amber Discko, Gabriela Barkho, and the team at *Femsplain* for first publishing me. I learned so much about writing and community from that experience.

I'm thankful to Mark Baumgarten for giving me a career and letting me live out my teenage *Almost Famous* dreams, and to my lovely editors during my time at *Seattle Weekly*. To Gwendolyn Elliott, who on my last day gifted me *My Body Is a Book of Rules* by Elissa Washuta, the book that ultimately inspired me to write this book and gave me permission to be weird. And to Kelton Sears for just generally being the coolest and saying I was the best intern they'd ever had. Sorry past and future *Seattle Weekly* interns.

Thank you to Kristen Millares Young for workshopping the most difficult essay in this book with me, and for being the first important writer-person who understood immediately what I was trying to do and encouraged me to keep going.

I owe so much to Kelsey Sipple. You are this book's guardian angel. Thank you for reading the very first drafts of the very first essays in this book and everything after. You read generously and you edit gracefully. You have beautiful instincts. And you're always right.

To Linda Barsi, you are a genius and probably the best editor out there. Thank you for making me and this book better. For telling me the mean manuscript consultant lady was wrong, that I could be weirder, and that I am close to my trauma but in the best way. I needed to hear that.

This book in its final form would not have been possible without my amazing team. Thank you to Daniela Olaru for the gorgeous cover illustration. No one does sad, hot girls quite like you. Willy Eddy, thank you for designing the cover and for always being the most fun to collaborate with both in and outside of work. Thank you to Taylor Rubright for copyediting and fixing my tenses without erasing my voice. Thank you to my layout designer Taylor Roy, for making it all look beautiful and effortless.

A big thank you to my cousin Dat for holding my hand through the business creation process. Let me know when you write that book.

I will forever be grateful to Katee and her family for giving me a place to land. I honestly don't know where I would be without that. I hope that I can pay you guys back one day.

Thank you to my family. Good, bad, and ugly, I wouldn't be here without you. To my younger sisters, Stephanie and Andrea, I look up to you both. Thank you for believing in me. To my brother Alex, you've always been my hero. Thank you for giving me good taste and guiding me from afar. To my mom, thank you for taking me to the library every week so I could max out my borrowing limit, and for bringing the newspaper I wrote as a kid to work and trying to sell it to your coworkers. I owe everything I have to you and the sacrifices that you've made. You've given me everything I need. And Bill, I want to thank you, too. Despite everything, I know I wouldn't be the strong, resilient, and hard-working person I am if not for what happened. You do have your good moments.

And lastly, to the little family I built. Bug, I loved growing up with you and being by you. Thank you for buying me Scrivener and giving me your blessing to write what needs to be written. And thank you to my cat, Slugbug, who I got when I was twelve and who is now seventeen. You've been through it all with me and we both made it out.

About the Author

Diana Le is the founder of Girl Noise Press. She's a recovering film major, turned music writer, turned copywriter. Her personal essays have appeared in *Femsplain*, *HelloGiggles*, and *Teen Vogue*. She lives in Seattle in an ethereal '80s teen grandma apartment.

■

girlnoise.net

Instagram: @girlnoise